Reading the Environment

Children's Literature in the Science Classroom

Mary M. Cerullo

HEINEMANN
Portsmouth, NH

HEINEMANN
A division of Reed Elsevier Inc.
361 Hanover Street
Portsmouth, NH 03801–3912

Offices and agents throughout the world

Library of Congress Cataloging-in-Publication Data
Cerullo, Mary.
    Reading the environment : children's literature in the science
classroom / Mary M. Cerullo.
        p.   cm.
    Includes bibliographical references.
    ISBN 0–435–08383–X (alk. paper)
    1. Science—Study and teaching (Elementary)—United States.
2. Children's literature—Study and teaching (Elementary)—United
States.   3. Environmental sciences—Study and teaching
(Elementary)—United States.   I. Title.
LB1585.3.C47   1997
372.3'5—dc21   97-8894
                                                                    CIP

Editors: Leigh Peake and Victoria Merecki
Production: Vicki Kasabian
Text and cover design: Joni Doherty
Cover illustration: Lindsay Duffy, kindergarten
Manufacturing: Louise Richardson

Printed in the United States of America on acid-free paper

01   00   99   98   97   EB   1   2   3   4   5

To Susan Sedenka,
exemplary teacher and friend

Contents

Acknowledgments

I wish to thank Alan Lishness of the Gulf of Maine Aquarium, Portland, Maine, and Thomas Clark of the Maine Mathematics and Science Alliance for permission to adapt materials that I had developed for their publications. The idea for this book emerged from workshops I taught as an educational consultant for the American Institute for Creative Education. Thanks also to Barbara Pullen and to the teachers who enriched my learning. And a special thank-you goes to Lindsay Duffy for her penguin drawing, which she drew in Mrs. Mary Burns's kindergarten class at Small School in South Portland, Maine.

1 *Why Science and Literature Belong Together*

Science is something children, especially younger ones, do naturally like throwing stones to make ripples in a pond, making leaf collections in the fall, or blowing milk bubbles through a straw. From a toddler's first "Why?" children are irrepressibly inquisitive about the natural world around them. Research studies have shown that when children are asked what they would prefer to study, they choose science more than half the time (Mechling and Kepler 1991).

Science trade books, both fiction and nonfiction, nurture a child's personal journey of discovery through the anecdotes, adventures, and experiences of others, and through vivid word and picture images. Lee Anne Stiffler writes in *Science and Children* (1992), "Science trade books help children see science as a part of their daily lives, not as something found only in a laboratory, classroom, or textbook." Literature-based science first engages our imagination and then challenges us to seek further, test the truth, and expand on the experiences in the story. Through literature, that exploration can extend well beyond the few hours during the school week formally devoted to "Science."

Combining literature and hands-on science activities helps spark the curiosity and excitement that, as Maine Teacher of the Year Bob Maurais says, "turn passive learners into principal investigators." By tackling a few subjects in depth and starting with what intrigues children, trade books overcome some of the complaints about elementary science textbooks (like trying to cover too much material superficially and not building on students' prior knowledge). Science trade books engage students' interest on both the intellectual and the emotional levels: this is why both fiction and nonfiction books belong in a science curriculum. Reading a fiction book aloud can be an evocative and compelling way to introduce a topic. The demise of a leaf, for example, in *The Fall of Freddie the Leaf* by Leo Buscaglia, is a personal and poignant way to begin a discussion of seasonal cycles.

Geologist and science writer Chet Raymo goes so far as to argue that fiction books—rather than factual science books for children—better develop the habits of mind that make good scientists by stimulating children's curiosity and imagination (Eggerton 1996). However, I believe that in a literature-rich science classroom, there is room for reference books, field guides, biographies, magazine articles, experiment and how-to books, poetry, and fiction books. Using trade books isn't intended to replace the reading program, but to complement it by adding engaging reading materials to inspire reflection and writing.

Oral reading of a storybook, a biography of a scientist, or a descriptive passage from a nonfiction book can make an intriguing introduction to a science topic. Or students may explore a new topic on their own by having access to a variety of science books in their reading center for silent reading time. Sometimes a current newspaper article can generate a heated discussion on the pros and cons of a particular issue (Lapp and Flood 1992). Any of these approaches can raise questions and issues for further investigation.

As students explore a subject further, more reference books are needed to provide the background to research in depth and to compare statements by different authors. A supply of both fiction and nonfiction sources will give children the information necessary to complete a science unit with a literary effort of their own. Reading aloud a fiction book or poems can also close a study of a topic. Other culminating projects might include a class project that emulates the style of a favorite author or illustrator, such as Joanna Cole and Bruce Degan of the *Magic School Bus* series or a visit by a science author or illustrator allowing the students to show off their knowledge to their guest.

Why Do Science and Literature Belong Together?

How would you rather study the rock cycle: by reading a textbook written in 1979, or by traveling to the center of the earth aboard Ms. Frizzle's Magic School Bus? Most students would vote for joining Joanna Cole, Ms. Frizzle's alter ego, or Seymour Simon, Patricia Lauber, or a host of other authors who know how to make science sizzle. Today's young people, raised in a visually rich culture of television and video games, aren't easily engaged by dry textbooks. Today's science trade books, with their lively texts and dramatic photos or paintings, lure young explorers into their pages. Once you have their attention, you can then communicate lessons in both science and language arts. Linking the two subjects not only gives you more time for both, it offers other learning opportunities as well.

Combining science and literature helps children explain events they observe

Science is the attempt to explain the cause and effect of natural events taking place around us. Scientific inquiry is part of our personal experience as well as our cultural past. Early civilizations attempted to explain their world by creating legends and superstitions, by telling stories. The Penobscot Indians of northern New England, for example, had a host of creation stories based on a godlike giant named Gluscap. Gluscap made the earth, the animals, his people, and the corn to feed them. Gluscap, according to one legend, fashioned the fishes from dirt and breathed life into them to populate the rivers and the sea. The first few fishes he made were crude and ugly, but he improved with practice. One day, just as Gluscap had finished his most perfect fish yet, his evil twin stomped it flat. That, according to legend, is how the flounder came to be.

Like ancient cultures, children make up their own theories to explain the processes around them. Every day, without instruction, children are learning about their environment by observing, making connections, and drawing conclusions, sometimes very original ones. "I can tell when it's noon," a teacher overheard one boy saying to his friend, "but how do you know when it's midnight?" "That's easy!" replied the other. "It's when the darkness is directly overhead!"

When children record their theories or creation stories, they create literature. When I was small, I wrote a story for my parents explaining "how the starfish came to be." A generation later, my daughter wrote about "why black bears are black" and "why flowers have petals." Children can find inspiration in books like Sandy Shepherd's *Myths and Legends from Around the World*, a rich compendium of "how the world began" legends from Japan, New Zealand, Tahiti, Scandinavia, and North America.

Combining science and literature helps children practice problem-solving skills

A well-written story usually involves resolving a conflict; science usually involves solving a problem. They use many of the same elements: observing carefully, defining the problem, framing useful questions, creating experiments or designing theories or solutions, gathering, selecting, and analyzing data, testing more than one solution, justifying strategies. Science may go beyond finding the solution to one problem by applying similar strategies and solutions to new situations (a strategy also employed by oft-published mystery writers). Both genres attempt to answer, *Who, What, Where, When,* and most important, *How* and *Why?*

Exposing children to science and literature helps develop recording skills

With trade books, students begin to recognize scientists as writers and storytellers. Whether as a written narrative in a scientific journal, scientific notation in a field journal, or a lecture to colleagues, scientists have to communicate and defend their results. Literature stimulates writing and communicating skills by showing the many ways information can be conveyed.

Combining science and literature helps children correct science misconceptions

Students frequently have erroneous, but strongly held, beliefs about science that can interfere with their absorbing the correct information. Children's literature, reinforced with hands-on activities, can help them counteract their confusion as they make real-world connections and applications that dispel their misconceptions. Repetition of the correct concept by reading several books, doing a number of experiments, and inviting scientists to the classroom can facilitate a conceptual change in children (Miller, Steiner, and Larson 1996).

Being introduced to science and literature helps children understand how science has affected human history

Many recent science trade books, particularly those with environmental themes, emphasize the connection between science issues and social responsibility. For instance, books like Jane Yolen's *Letting Swift River Go*, about the drowning of several Massachusetts towns to create a water supply for Boston, and Lynne Cherry's *A River Ran Wild*, an environmental history of the Nashua River, illustrate how humans have altered not only the health but also the very course of natural systems.

Exposing children to science and literature helps them appreciate that science is dynamic

By comparing different trade books, particularly newer books to older ones, students can see how science is changing. Science is not a collection of static facts but a fluid field of inquiry that is constantly undergoing revision and updating. Current trade books communicate the message that, though we have made astonishing progress in the last century, these new discoveries often raise more questions than answers.

Combining science and literature helps children understand that science can be serendipitous

One of the most compelling aspects of studying science is that you are never quite sure where it will take you. In fact, some great (and not-so-great) inventions and scientific discoveries were the result of "failed" experiments. Consider the fact that penicillin, Post-It Notes, and Silly Putty were all discovered by chance. Scientists who followed these detours made exciting new inroads in science, sometimes using information that other scientists had ignored.

Lucky Science: Accidental Discoveries from Gravity to Velcro by Roylston M. Roberts and Jeanie Roberts recounts the stories of twenty scientific breakthroughs that were discovered by accident, plus experiments that illustrate them.

Children can experience being scientists, sleuths, and explorers

Science literature—informational books, biographies, and even fiction—provides role models for students and lets them imagine themselves in the role of scientist, explorer, and discoverer. Mark Taylor's *Henry the Explorer* series from Atheneum features a young Canadian boy who organizes expeditions with his canine companion, Laird Angus McAngus, to explore the impenetrable jungle, the Orinoco River, or whatever new destination that has captured Henry's imagination. Henry's adventures exemplify what draws real scientists to their journeys of discovery.

Sylvia Earle's solo descent to the bottom of the sea and Bob Ballard's discovery of the sunken *Titanic* read like adventure stories, which, in fact, they are. Books that personalize scientists and their work show students that science is an accessible and exciting field.

What Is the Scientific Method?

Science trade books introduce students to the concepts of the scientific method: observing, formulating a hypothesis, gathering and recording data to test that hypothesis, analyzing, and drawing a conclusion. Bonnie Armbruster of the University of Illinois wrote in 1993 in *The Reading Teacher*

> The same skills that make good scientists also make good readers: engaging prior knowledge, forming hypotheses, establishing plans, evaluating understanding, determining the relative importance of information, describing patterns, comparing and contrasting, making inferences, generalizing, evaluating sources, and so on.

What are the stages of the scientific process?

There are no fixed, irrevocable steps in the scientific process; it is rather like a clover leaf where you can double back on yourself in several places. Ultimately, with luck and perseverence, this leads to new knowledge, however circuitously. Books illustrate various stages in the scientific process. At any time during an investigation a scientist (child or adult) may go back to other steps, but in general the sequence goes like this:

1. Make an observation. In *Digging up Tyrannosaurux* Rex by Jack Horner and Don Lessem, the discovery of the bones of a big animal by rancher Kathy Wankel leads to a major discovery.

2. Ask a question. In *The Pebble in My Pocket* by Meredith Hooper, a little girl asks "Where did you come from, pebble?"

3. Design an experiment to collect facts, samples, or data. Starting with a shovel and a bucket and advancing to a magma-proof, jet-propelled submarine, two young boys invent imaginative ways to find out *How to Dig a Hole to the Other Side of the World* by Faith McNulty.

4. Interpret data. In *Signs Along the River,* Kayo Robertson challenges us to deduce who or what may have left footprints, slide marks, and other clues along a river's edge.

5. Come to a conclusion. This step often leads to new questions. In *The News About Dinosaurs* by Patricia Lauber recently unearthed evidence leads scientists to rethink and adapt old ideas about dinosaurs.

The books mentioned for each step can help you encourage children in learning about the scientific method or a step of the process. Some teachers post the steps of the scientific process so children can refer to them occasionally. As they read these and other books, they have the students analyze how the authors or scientists in the books made use of the scientific process.

What Is It That We Want Young Minds to Absorb About Science?

Recent reports on the status of science education warn that

> It is no longer possible for teachers to "cover the facts" of science, given that the production of new scientific and technological information is expanding exponentially. The process skills of science, however, contain some useful techniques for survival in our increasingly complex world. (Commission on Maine's Common Core of Learning 1990)

This statement suggests that it is no longer relevant just to convey facts and figures (some of which may already be outdated anyway). But what if, like many elementary teachers, you aren't so sure what those science facts are to begin with? How do you insert science into the language arts curriculum if you aren't a science specialist? Take heart from science writer Patricia Lauber's confession before a convention of English teachers: "Science was never one of my interests in school or college; in fact, I might go so far as to say I never met a science course I liked" (1992). I suspect the fault was not with Patricia Lauber, whose *Volcano: The Eruption and Healing of Mt. St. Helens* was a Newbery Honor Book, but with the less-than-inspiring instruction she received during her academic career. It wasn't until she became an editor of a science magazine for high school students that she discovered she actually enjoyed learning about

> How discoveries in science had affected the way we live and the way we think about social issues and how all these changes are reflected in our literature. . . . Overall, my aims are to help children understand how the earth (or its parts) works and to try to imbue them with some of my own sense of wonderment in the hope that they will grow up to be good stewards, who will take care of the earth, not just use (or abuse) it. (1992)

If we can foster that same attitude in our students, our science curriculum will be a success. Along with enthusiasm and excitement, if we arm young people with the scientific method and an inquiry approach to reasoning and problem solving, we will have given them the tools to become "principal investigators" on their own. How better than through literature to inspire Sherlock Holmes's passion for science, to view science as a journey of discovery, a search for truth. How wonderful it would be to spark that excitement in our classroom that Holmes emotes as he leaps from his chair and cries, "Come, Watson, the game's afoot!"

By integrating literature, personal observation, and hands-on exploration, we have the best chance of engaging our youngsters in science discovery. We don't need to be brilliant like Holmes. We just need to remember that even scientists don't have all the answers, and they can't always agree on the ones they think they have.

What Is It We Mean by Scientific Literacy?

In the mid-1980s, a growing concern about the lack of science understanding among most Americans spurred panels of scientists, engineers, mathematicians, historians, educators, and others to define what it meant to be "scientifically literate." They developed a set of recommendations on what all citizens should understand about science, mathematics, and technology in order to be able to think for themselves and participate in a world increasingly shaped by science and technology. Ultimately, more than 400 individuals contributed to *Science for All Americans*, a 1990 report by the American Association for the Advancement of Science (AAAS), on the meaning of scientific literacy. It describes the skills and ideas a person should know by the time she graduates from high school:

> Scientific literacy . . . include[s] being familiar with the natural world and respecting its unity; being aware of some of the important ways in which mathematics, technology, and the sciences depend upon one another; understanding some of the key concepts and principles of science; having a capacity for scientific ways of thinking; knowing that science, mathematics, and technology are human enterprises, and knowing what that implies about their strengths and limitations; and being able to use scientific knowledge and ways of thinking for personal and social purposes.

A companion book, *Benchmarks for Science Literacy*, was published in 1993. *Benchmarks* maps out the components of scientific literacy that students should acquire sequentially over thirteen years of education. It lists 855 benchmarks—or statements—of what all students should know or be able to do in science, mathematics, and technology by the end of grades 2, 5, 8, and 12.

Notice that half of the phrase *scientific literacy* is *literacy*. Mary Ann Brearton, who helps teachers learn to use the *Benchmarks for Science Literacy*, explained in a presentation to math and science educators on September 4, 1996, that

> Clear communication is an essential part of doing science. It enables scientists to inform others about their work, expose their ideas to criticism by other scientists, and stay informed about science discoveries around the world.

Like the *National Science Educations Standards* published in 1996 by the National Research Council, *Benchmarks* encourages "inquiry science." As sixth-grade teacher Debra C. Breger explains in the October 1995 issue of *Science Scope*, "Science originates with and is guided by inquiry. Learning to ask the right questions and to learn through reading will lead to further investigations and wise decision making." In the same issue of *Science Scope*, University of Georgia professor Mary M. Atwater professes that, "[Students] do not merely retrieve information, but fuse their new and old knowledge in many ways. Science investigations furnish meaningful contexts to enhance students' reading, writing, speaking, and listening knowledge." So scientists, college professors, and classroom teachers agree: Science and literature belong together!

Linking the Science Curriculum to Current Environmental Issues

Just as educators are combining science and literature to present an integrated approach to learning, researchers, especially in the environmental sciences, are beginning to take an integrated approach to science. A quarter century ago, when I was studying to become a scientist (which I never did), science was highly compartmentalized. The further one advanced academically, the more specialized one became in one's field. Now, with an ecosystem approach, biologists, chemists, geologists, physicists, mathematicians, engineers, and computer technologists often cooperate to study such broad questions as global warming or the Gulf Stream's movements. Researchers who several years ago would have had little to discuss at a faculty Christmas party are now writing grant proposals together. Increasingly, science is also becoming linked with social problems, such as damage to coral reefs or watershed pollution.

As humans change the environment to meet the needs of an expanding population, they can create unforeseen stresses on the environment. For instance, cutting down forests for lumber or opening up the land for farming often causes topsoil to be washed downstream, muddying streams or even smothering delicate corals on near-shore reefs. Understanding how natural systems operate, including human systems, is a lot more complex than one discipline can address.

This integrated approach in the environmental sciences is one reason why this area of science works so well with students. Linking the science curriculum to ongoing issues makes the subject more real and relevant to learners. Mary M. Atwater, in the October 1995 issue of *Science Scope*, asserts,

> An understanding of scientific principles is important for making decisions on many issues. . . . by investigating a topic from different perspectives, they achieve a balanced point of view that will serve them when they become adults making decisions vital to the future of their families, their country, and their world.

Fieldwork, experimentation, and the observation of natural phenomena are also easier in the environmental sciences than in other areas of study such as pathology or microbiology. Finally, the environmental sciences are subjects about which students are usually naturally curious. Most students are self-appointed naturalists who observe and explore on their own. It only requires a small nudge of encouragement and reinforcement to nurture that curiosity so it thrives past elementary school.

Like Russian dolls, living systems are nested within other living systems, each interdependent with the other. According to the Center for Ecoliteracy, all ecological cycles act as "feedback loops" so that the biological community regulates itself and maintains an overall balance. An ecosystem is made up of all the living things in it as well as the physical factors that affect them, including the soil, water, air, nutrients, energy, and climate. For a comprehensive description of concepts in environmental education, refer to *Essential Learnings in Environmental Education* published by the North American Association for Environmental Education (Ballard and Pandya 1990). This reference states that the earth is made up of four layers or spheres: the *atmosphere* (air), the *hydrosphere* (water), the *lithosphere* (land and underground), and the *biosphere* (life). The trade books and activities suggested in this book touch on each of these aspects of the earth and its ecology.

The environmental topics in the following chapters share these overarching themes of patterns in nature: *cycles, constancy and change, systems,* and *connectedness.* In subsequent chapters, we will be looking at these themes through studies of weather, seasons, water cycles, watersheds, food webs, adaptations, and rock cycles.

Each chapter begins with an overview of specific themes or central ideas, followed by suggested books and activities that illustrate those ideas. This is not meant to be a "cookbook" of lesson plans linked to specific readings. I've tried to devote more attention to the "why" than to the "how to." I hope the suggested books and activity ideas will lead to questions that inspire other activities and other questions, just as good science does.

Criteria for Selecting a Science Trade Book

Trade books are a valuable resource for the elementary teacher, as reference, reinforcement, or inspiration for a science lesson. When you are choosing trade books for your classroom library, you might ask yourself the same kinds of questions editors and publishers anguish over before they release a new title: Is the format appealing? Would a teacher, parent, or grandparent choose this book? Will a child read this book?

Check the table of contents and the index to see if there are any obvious gaps in information. Read the first few pages to determine if it is well written in a style that is interesting and accessible. Do the illustrations or photos and captions stand on their own? Do they help explain and extend the text?

Skim through the entire book to see if it is accurate. If you don't feel qualified to decide, ask a colleague, a librarian, or look up a book review about it in a literary magazine such as those listed at the end of this chapter. You can check the author's credentials highlighted in the biography on the jacket flap. The acknowledgments will indicate whether the author consulted experts while researching or writing the manuscript.

Does it engage the reader?

If the book's not interesting, it won't be read. Nonfiction writer John McFee once commented, "Whatever you're writing, your motive is to tell a good story while you're sitting around the cave, in front of the fire, before going out to club another mastodon" (Freedman 1992). An author should have a storyteller's talent for grabbing and holding the audience's attention. Many times authors seek to do that from the first sentence, as in *Tentacles* by James Martin: "In 1872, a schooner was sailing on the Indian Ocean when two giant tentacles emerged from the water," and in *Sharks: Challengers of the Deep:* "A rigid dorsal fin slices through the water and within seconds the cry of 'Shark!' clears the beach."

For me, the test of a great novel is whether I wonder about what happens to the characters after I turn the last page. The test of a great piece of science literature is if it motivates its readers to keep exploring that and other subjects of science after they finish the book.

Is it accurate?

Oftentimes, discrepancies that appear in different books on the same subject can be attributed to the fact that scientists honestly disagree about many issues. These differences make great fodder for classroom discussions, such as Do fish see color? Were dinosaurs really cold-blooded? How intelligent are cats? Also, in writing children's books, authors by necessity have to condense and simplify a subject. They may have to leave out the exceptions to the rule and make some generalizations. Scientists hate to deal in absolutes like *always, every,* or *never.* Authors can respect this by using phrases like "many scientists believe" or "in most cases" to qualify their statements.

In some cases, the facts in a book may just be wrong. One children's book explains that a starfish eats by drilling a hole through its victim's shell (moon snails do; starfish pull open the shells). In another popular children's book, the illustration of the entrance to the wise old beaver's lodge is above the waterline. Such errors can be turned into a learning opportunity for children to point out where an author, illustrator, or editor has gone wrong. South Portland, Maine, teacher Mary Burns had her multiage class write thank-you notes after a visit from the author of the beaver story. In their letters, several students pointed out the mistake in her book.

Accuracy also implies providing a balanced presentation about a topic. Most authors of informational books strive to present diverse viewpoints, even though they may not weigh them equally. After all, it is the privilege of authors to portray their prejudices, as long as they admit that openly. As Laurence Pringle says, "My voice is not a bland, neutral one, with equal weight and space given to opposing interests, and I avoid any claims to strict objectivity" (Bosma 1992). If the teacher provides several books on the same subject, students can compare authors' voices and decide which claims they support.

Is it clearly written?

Children's author Russell Freedman recounts that, "Franklyn Branley has said that it is only when he must explain a subject to children that he realizes he doesn't understand it at all" (Freedman 1992). A good author gathers all the facts and then distills them down to a clear, concise picture. This is a corollary to the teacher's adage, "You never know how well you understand something until you have to teach it."

Is it up-to-date?

One of the most compelling attributes of science is that it is always changing (or at least our understanding of it is). Theories and convictions held even twenty years ago have been disproved and revised as science advances. One of the most important messages I try to convey to children about science is that they may well make discoveries that will change the assumptions we hold about science today. Therefore, a danger in using older science literature is that some of the "facts" may no longer be true.

A book that beautifully illustrates the evolution in scientific thinking is Patricia Lauber's *The News About Dinosaurs*. The author shows how new discoveries refute old assumptions about dinosaurs, first by discussing a long-held theory, such as that dinosaurs were clumsy, lumbering beasts. Below it, she presents "The News" that, after analyzing dinosaur footprints, scientists now believe many dinosaurs were quick and agile.

Does it avoid stereotypes?

Older science books also tend to reinforce stereotypes about scientists. Yarmouth, Maine, teacher Gordon Corbett began his science course each year by asking his sixth graders to help him draw a picture of a scientist on the blackboard. The students usually suggested an image of a white male with glasses, clad in a lab coat, with pens and a calculator poking out of his pocket. Then Gordon would unveil a photo of underwater explorer Sylvia Earle decked out in a bikini and scuba gear. "Could this be a scientist?" he would ask. His middle-school students instantly revised their image of what a scientist ought to look like.

Newer books usually include images of both men and women researchers of different races. With the goal of encouraging science as a career choice for women and minorities, it is an idea that can use frequent repetition.

Is it anthropomorphic?

Strict constructionists disparage anthropomorphism in science literature. They worry that children will be confused by attributing human shapes or characteristics to animals, plants, or inanimate things. While children (and authors) sometimes give animals more credit for higher thinking skills like planning and problem solving than they deserve, students can generally distinguish fact from fantasy. But it's good to make sure—Joanna Cole, author of The Magic School Bus series, is careful to point out what is real and what is not at the end of each book. One way to begin a discussion of a book they've just read is to ask students, "What was fact and what was make-believe?"

While a fiction book can contain talking animals and plants, attributing human characteristics to them, a nonfiction book should not, as a rule, be either *anthropomorphic* or *teleological,* which attempts to assign humanlike purposes to plants, animals, and natural phenomena. For example, a turtle does not sit on a log because it *enjoys* basking in the sun, a shark does not attack a human *out of malice,* nor does the rain fall *in order* to bring relief to parched lands.

Does it need to be at grade level?

As long as a student is interested in a subject, the reading level of the book is less important than its content. Beginning readers may just look up the pictures and the name of a species, skipping the descriptions in an adult-level field guide. A more advanced chapter book, like *Newberry: The Life and Times of a Maine Clam* by Vincent Dethier, could be read aloud after lunch to early grades. Even very young students can appreciate its wry humor and the occasional line drawings of its bivalve hero wrapped in a purple muffler. On the other hand, a storybook can be a welcome change of pace for older students. I know a high school teacher who reads aloud to his students. He says they love it.

Some children's science stories defy being classified for younger or older students. *Pagoo, Minn of the Mississippi,* and *Paddle-to-the-Sea* by Holling Clancey Holling are so thoroughly researched that they could be used as middle-school texts in either science or social studies.

When I'm initially researching a science topic I plan to write about for either adults or children, I start in the children's section of the library. The books there tend to explain the subject more clearly, get straight to the salient facts, and omit extraneous material that may be of more interest to the scientist than to the layperson. Only after I have built my foundation do I go to the adult section or to the scientific literature in a university library. If I plan to interview a scientist, I make sure to check out several beginning books on the subject so I won't waste her time asking questions I could have easily answered myself.

Is it organized well?

A fiction book should have a beginning, a middle, and an end, and so should a nonfiction book. Beyond that, an informational book should be organized for easy reference with a table of contents, chapters and subheads, as well as an index, appendix, or glossary, and suggestions for further reading. A bibliography, ideally, should be divided into annotated adult and juvenile references.

Librarian Toni Bennett runs a book-review club with the second graders at the Lyseth School in Portland, Maine. When discussing nonfiction trade books for review in their school newspaper, one of the criteria they consider is whether the book covers the topic in a comprehensive manner. "How many questions do you still have left after reading the book?" she asks the students.

Trends in Children's Literature in Science

Beginning in the 1980s, an explosion in the publishing of children's books has generated close to five thousand new titles each year (Elleman 1992). Many of these are in nonfiction literature, which now makes up about 30 percent of the books in children's sections of bookstores and approximately 70 percent of school libraries (Dowd 1992). With parents actively supporting and supplementing their children's education at home, and trade books replacing textbooks in many schools, the popularity of trade books should continue to increase.

Provide opportunities for further exploration

Newer science trade books for children often include explanatory text after the story to provide more in-depth facts for parents and teachers (rather like "crib notes" for adults). For example, Bruce McMillan has included an exemplary explanation of whale behavior and biology at the end of his concept book, *Going on a Whale Watch*. Nonfiction books for older readers frequently contain a glossary, index, and bibliography that help extend learning.

Offer richer illustrations and photographs

Compared to twenty years ago, today's crop of science literature for children has made impressive advances in the areas of illustration and design. The quality of today's books reflects the fact that artists and photographers who used to focus on adult books are now entering the children's book market. Because of their proliferation and profitability, children's books have gained a new status in publishing houses. Although children's book awards still seem to favor fiction, nonfiction science books are beginning to be recognized more frequently.

Are more creatively engaging

In addition to their colorful images, many books use attention-getting devices like pop-up figures, sliding windows, or creative design and illustration techniques to stand out from other children's books. One of the most innovative ones is A. J. Wood's *A Night in the Dinosaur Graveyard*, which features "ten spooky holograms" of dinosaurs. In *A River Ran Wild*, a border of small, meticulously researched images (à la Jan Brett) surround the main story. They illustrate ideas that expand and complement the text, such as Indian artifacts, settlers' tools, native animals, and the stages of a campaign to rehabilitate the river. Analyzing these small illustrations is a student project in itself.

Another graphic technique is the use of predictive illustrations to alert the reader to what is coming up on the next page. In *Animal Fact: Animal Fable* by Seymour Simon, the reader sees an illustration of a commonly accepted aphorism such as, "A porcupine shoots its quills" or "Bulls get angry when they see red." He must turn the page to find out the true facts. This book is also a good lead-in to a discussion about common misconceptions in science.

Some books turn into something else. *Build Your Own Rainforest* and *Build Your Own Coral Reef* convert into free-standing, three-dimensional models of these ecosystems. After they read the text, children can transform the book *Incredible Model Dinosaurs* by Charles Peattie and Phil Healey into ten freestanding paper dinosaurs.

Don't talk down to children

Some children's books sound as if the authors are directing themselves to an adult reading over the child's shoulder. This might be because these authors are used to writing for adults, or they may not understand the material sufficiently well to pare it down to a simpler level, or they may be too conscientious to do so. Occasionally you will see a trade book whose language seems geared to adults, but whose large type and bountiful illustrations indicate the intended audience is children.

On the plus side, today's children's books rarely talk down to children. They respect their audience. They tend to be thoroughly researched, they don't avoid large words and sophisticated concepts, and they deal with serious issues and current events like pollution and extinction that once were only the realm of adult literature. After a recent massive oil spill in my community, I turned to a Let's-Read-and-Find-Out Science book, *Oil Spill!* by Melvin Berger, for a concise explanation of oil cleanup methods that were cited but unexplained in the local newspaper.

The science topics I am focusing on are commonly found in elementary science programs: earth science, weather and seasons, water cycles and watersheds, and the ocean. All of these illustrate the environmental themes of cycles, constancy and change, systems, and connectedness. In each chapter I have tried to provide

- Background information, such as discussions of current scientific knowledge or explanations of terms
- Brief summaries of relevant trade books
- Hands-on science activities
- Suggestions for class discussion
- Student writing activities, and
- Bibliography of books mentioned in that chapter.

In addition to the books and ideas I suggest, you will want to evaluate other books and hands-on activities. There are a wealth of resources to help you.

Help for Teachers

There are many sources to turn to for help in selecting suitable science trade books and supporting curriculum materials. They include:

Book Reviews:
- *School Library Journal*
- *The Horn Book Guide* (published 6 times a year)
- *Booklist* (published twice a month by American Library Association)

- *Appraisal: Children's Science Books for Young People,* a quarterly publication of the Children's Science Book Review Committee, 605 Commonwealth Ave., Boston, MA 02215. It has paired reviews written by a librarian and a scientist.
- *Science and Children,* published by the National Science Teachers Association
- *Science Books and Films*
- *Learning*
- *Encounters: Explorations of Science*

Many, though not all, use reviewers who are knowledgeable in the field. Frequently, the reviewer's credentials are decribed.

Recommended Book Lists:

- *American Bookseller Pick of the Lists* often includes science books.
- *Outstanding Science Trade Books for Children,* published in the March issue of *Science and Children,* selected by National Science Teachers Association and Children's Book Council.
- *Orbis Pictus Outstanding Nonfiction Books for Children,* published by the National Council of Teachers of English (NCTE).

Bibliographies by Theme:

- *Book Links: Connecting Books, Libraries, and Classrooms,* published six times a year by *Booklist* of the American Library Association. Each issue features a bibliography on a different subject area to integrate selected children's books into the curriculum.
- *Nature's Course,* a quarterly publication of the Center for Children's Environmental Literature (CCEL), P.O. Box 5995, Washington, DC 20016. Each issue focuses on a different environmental topic. Back issues on oceans, rivers, and more are available. CCEL was founded by Lynne Cherry, author of *The Great Kapok Tree* and *A River Ran Wild.*
- Sinclair, P. 1992. *E Is for Environment: An Annotated Bibliography of Children' Books with Environmental Themes,* New Providence, NJ: R.R. Bowker.
- *Bringing the World Alive: A Bibliography of Nature Stories for Children,* published by Orion Society, 136 East 64th Street, New York, NY 10021. It lists picture books that "reflect and celebrate the realm of the child and the natural world."

Environmental and Educational Organizations:

- National Audubon Society, 700 Broadway, New York, New York 10003, as well as state Audubon Societies.

- National Wildlife Federation (creator *of Ranger Rick Magazine* and *Nature Scope,* an exemplary environmental curriculum series), 1412 16th Street, NW, Washington, DC 20036–2266.

- National Science Teachers Association, 1742 Connecticut Avenue, NW, Washington, DC 20009.

- North American Association for Environmental Education, P.O. Box 400, Troy, Ohio 45373.

- National Maine Educators Association, J.L. Scott Marine Education Center & Gulf Coast Research Laboratory, P.O. Box 7000, Ocean Springs, MS 39566–7000.

Other Resources:

- Science museums, zoos, and aquariums all have relevant curriculum materials, books, and kits for sale or loan.

- Nature magazines for reference: *Ranger Rick's Nature Magazine, School Bulletin, Zoobooks, 3-2-1 Contact, National Geographic World, Kids Discover, Science World, Cricket,* and *Garbage,* as well as adult magazines such as *National Geographic, National and International Wildlife* (they alternate issues), *ZooWorld, Audubon Magazine, Earth, Discover, Odyssey,* and so forth.

- Nature guides, such as *Peterson Field Guides* (Houghton Mifflin) initiated by Roger Tory Peterson in 1934, provide scientific illustrations for identification while *Audubon Society Field Guides* (Knopf) use color photographs. *Stokes Nature Guides* (Little, Brown), which are not meant as comprehensive identification guides, do offer insightful observations of animal behavior and life cycles. *The Field Guides to Wildlife Habitats of Eastern and Western United States* (Fireside) group animals by habitat. *Golden Guides* (Golden Press), under the guidance of Dr. Herbert S. Zim, are still among the best buys in introductory field guides, with adequate illustrations and good explanations.

Children's Books Cited

Ballard, Robert. 1990. *The Discovery of the* Titanic. Avenal, NJ: Random House Value Publishing.

———. 1991. *Exploring the* Titanic. New York: Scholastic.

BAYLOR, BYRD. 1980. *If You Are a Hunter of Fossils.* New York: Scribner Books for Young Readers.

BERGER, MELVIN. 1994. *Oil Spill!* New York: HarperCollins Children's Books.

BUSCAGLIA, LEO. 1982. *The Fall of Freddie the Leaf: A Story of Life for All Ages.* New York: Henry Holt & Company.

CERULLO, MARY. 1993. *Sharks: Challengers of the Deep.* New York: Cobblehill Books.

CHERRY, LYNNE. 1992. *A River Ran Wild: An Environmental History.* San Diego: Harcourt Brace Juvenile Books.

COLE, JOANNA. 1986. *The Magic School Bus at the Waterworks.* New York: Scholastic.

———. 1989. *The Magic School Bus Inside the Earth.* New York: Scholastic.

CONLEY, ANDREA. 1991. *Window on the Deep: The Adventures of Underwater Explorer Sylvia Earle.* New York: Franklin Watts.

DETHIER, VINCENT. 1981. *Newberry: The Life and Times of a Maine Clam.* Camden, ME: Down East Books.

HOLLING, HOLLING C. 1980. *Paddle-to-the-Sea.* Boston: Houghton Mifflin.

———. 1957, 1990. *Pagoo.* Boston: Houghton Mifflin.

———. 1978, 1992. *Minn of the Missippi.* Boston: Houghton Mifflin.

HOOPER, MEREDITH, and CHRIS COADY. 1996. *The Pebble in My Pocket: A History of Our Earth.* New York: Viking.

HORNER, JACK, and DON LESSEM. 1992. *Digging up Tyrannosaurus Rex.* New York: Crown Books for Young Readers.

LAUBER, PATRICIA. 1986. *Volcano: The Eruption and Healing of Mt. St. Helens.* New York: Bradbury Press.

———. 1989. *The News About Dinosaurs.* New York: Bradbury Press.

MARTIN, JAMES. 1993. *Tentacles: Octopus, Squid, and Their Relatives.* New York: Crown Books for Young Readers.

MCMILLAN, BRUCE. 1992. *Going on a Whale Watch.* New York: Scholastic.

MCNULTY, FAITH. 1979. *How to Dig a Hole to the Other Side of the World.* New York: HarperCollins Children's Books.

PEATTIE, CHARLES, and PHIL HEALEY. 1994. *Incredible Model Dinosaurs.* Kansas City, MO: Andrews and McMeel.

ROBERTS, ROYLSTON, and JEANIE ROBERTS. 1995. *Lucky Science: Accidental Discoveries from Gravity to Velcro.* New York: John Wiley & Sons.

ROBERTSON, KAYO. 1986. *Signs Along the River: Learning to Read the Natural Landscape.* Boulder, CO: Roberts Rinehart Publishing Group.

SHEPHERD, SANDY. 1995. *Myths and Legends from Around the World.* New York: Macmillan Books for Young Readers.

SIMON, SEYMOUR. 1986. *Animal Fact: Animal Fable.* New York: Crown Books for Young Readers.

TAYLOR, MARK. 1966. *Henry the Explorer.* New York: Atheneum Books for Young Readers.

———. 1968. *Henry Explores the Jungle.* New York: Atheneum Books for Young Readers.

———. 1972. *Henry the Castaway.* New York: Atheneum Books for Young Readers.

———. 1975. *Henry Explores the Mountains.* New York: Atheneum Books for Young Readers.

WATSON, CAROL. 1993. *Build Your Own Rainforest.* New York: Lodestar Books.

WELLS, SUE. 1994. *Build Your Own Coral Reef.* New York: Lodestar Books.

WOOD, A. J. 1994. *A Night in the Dinosaur Graveyard.* New York: HarperCollins Children's Books.

YOLEN, JANE. 1992. *Letting Swift River Go.* Boston: Little, Brown.

2 Reading the Landscape: Earth Science

Earth science compels us to notice it because it's right under our feet. Reading stories and nonfiction can help a child learn to "read the rocks." Rocks go through changes and cycles, but most processes in earth science happen too slowly to observe firsthand, even in a lifetime. Books speed up the process so youngsters can understand concepts such as weathering and erosion, making rocks and fossils, plate tectonics, and building mountains and wearing them down. On the other hand, some catastrophic events such as earthquakes and volcanic eruptions happen so suddenly that they can only be documented later and at a safe distance in time and space.

Some of the lessons children can learn through literature on earth science include:

- The rock cycle, though infinitely slow compared to other cycles, can be traced through different kinds of rocks and landforms.
- Fossils help us read the earth's history.
- Some earth changes are rapid and catatrophic.
- Rocks and minerals impact all aspects of our lives.

Let's take a look at how children's literature can help students learn about the earth. Even though they may be far away from the action, children—through books—can see the changes that ice, wind, water, waves, earthquakes, and volcanoes can make to the landscape. They can journey to the center of the earth or back to the age of dinosaurs.

The rock cycle can be traced through different kinds of rocks and landforms.

Rocks are weathered and eroded over time by wind, water, and glaciers, reducing them to sand and soil. Eventually, the rock cycle buries the sand and soil in the earth's interior and transforms them into rock again. Rocks rise up into towering mountains and wear down into low hills or deep valleys. This process may take millions of years. Research on student understanding related in *Benchmarks for Science Literacy* (1993) says, "Students of all ages may hold the view that the world is always as it is now, or that any changes that have occurred must have been sudden and comprehensive." Books like *The Big Rock* and *The Pebble in My Pocket* help illustrate the long process of geologic change through erosion, deposition, and transformation.

Introducing Change

Earth science is the study of change. All things change, even something as immutable as a rock. Though children may be resistant to believing that boulders and mountains can change, you can start to ease them into accepting this concept by inviting them to notice how they have changed and how their immediate world around them changes. Ask students, "How do you know you change?" Ask them to bring in photos of themselves as toddlers. Mount the pictures, without identifying names, on a bulletin board, and have the class try to identify their classmates.

You can also ask students, "How could you learn about changes in your neighborhood?" (Possible answers: We see them, we talk to people, we could read old newspapers, we could look at old photos or maps, and so on.) Invite learners to interview an elderly neighbor or a grandparent to learn how the area has changed since these longtime residents were small. Have them ask how the landscape has changed as well.

Several wordless picture books help demonstrate how neighborhoods change. *Anno's USA* by Matsumasa Anno depicts different parts of the country at various periods in American history. *The Story of an English Village* by John S. Goodall shows the growth of an English village from a fourteenth-century medieval fortification to a congested modern city. *Window* by Jeannie Baker is a collection of paper-shape images of a community changing from rural to urban over the course of the boy's childhood. As seen through a boy's bedroom window, the countryside yields its trees and wildlife to billboards and buildings by the time the boy reaches adulthood. In the last image, the young man holds his newborn child at another window overlooking a country scene in which the encroaching city is still miles away. Nevertheless, the author expresses the hope that humans can control and protect our environment.

A more optimistic view of change is Lynne Cherry's *A River Ran Wild*, which shows children that human intervention can sometimes reverse environmental damage. Barbara Cooney's *Miss Rumphius* also provides a positive counterpoint that conveys the important message that one caring person can make a difference for the environment. It is the story of a remarkable woman who after a life of adventure recalls her father's admonition to make the world a better place. She does so by planting lupines all around her seaside community.

Before beginning a unit on earth science, fourth- and fifth-grade students were asked to draw two images: one depicting an "old" mountain and one of a "young" mountain. In many instances, the children depicted the old mountain as taller than the young mountain. They associated growing *up* with growing *older*. Although students can look at the earth (at least their part of it) as it is, they can't usually see geology as it *was*. For that reason, the study of earth science, perhaps more than most natural sciences, depends on books to help students travel back in time.

In *City Rocks, City Blocks, and the Moon*, Edward Gallob expresses the idea that geology is the study of change in a way every child can understand: "Geology is seashells becoming limestone, becoming marble, becoming the walls of your school building, or the steps you sit on." The earth is constantly changing, building up, wearing down, and re-creating itself. Some changes we can see in our lifetimes, such as the disappearance of beach sand—kidnapped by waves and ocean currents—from the front of a seaside cottage. Other changes we might not notice in a hundred years, like a boulder crumbling under the constant attack of wind, rain, and ice.

Earth science must try to solve the mystery of the earth's past using clues and evidence that may be millions of years old. Geologists are the investigators in a real-life detective story. They have to rely on some established beliefs, or geologic principles, such as "The present is the key to the past." This theory that the same processes operating in the present also operated in the past was first proposed by Scottish physician James Hutton in 1785. It contradicted the accepted belief at the time that geologic change was the result of rapid and catastrophic events like floods and earthquakes. He suggested instead that the landscape was shaped by gradual, constant changes over long periods of time through such processes as erosion and deposition. An outgrowth of this theory is that the earth must be very old in order to have enough time for these processes to take place. By observing events happening today, people can deduce what might have happened thousands, millions, and even billions of years ago.

One of the reasons that geology is such a good subject for study is that students can be as clever a sleuth as any adult. As long as they can offer a rational theory or explanation no one can prove them wrong since most of the geologic mysteries they are trying to solve took place long before there were any eyewitnesses.

Rock Collections

The study of geology can begin in your own backyard. Every child, it seems, has a rock collection. In *Everybody Needs a Rock*, Byrd Baylor offers her ten rules for finding the perfect rock. Her rules encourage children to use their senses—smell, touch, and sight—to make them aware of some of the same identifying characteristics that geologists use—weight, color, texture, shape. At the end, she invites her readers to come up with their own rules, which could be a natural classroom follow-up to reading this book.

For young students, you might want to begin a study of earth science with a discussion about, "What is a rock? Is it alive? Was it ever alive?" (No, but it may contain fossils.) "What are rocks good for?" (Possible answers: buildings, roads, statues, appreciation, jewelry, rock collections, and so on.)

Starting a classroom rock collection introduces students to the many variations in rocks. Either for homework or as a school-yard activity, have each child collect five rocks, using the ten (or more) rules derived from *Everybody Needs a Rock*. Students can permanently identify their individual rock specimens by placing two dots of white correction fluid or white enamel model paint on each rock sample, or "hand specimen," as geologists call it. With a fine-point indelible marker, a student puts his initials on one dot and the numbers 1–5 on the other dot. Have students record the numbers in a notebook and note where each rock was found, the date, and any details about the find. This way, youngsters can mix their rocks together and reclaim their own rocks later.

Perhaps you can set up a table to serve as a rock museum on which all the rocks are displayed together. Students may start to point out differences among their rocks right away, or they may group them together using their own criteria. To move the process along, you might ask, "What are the attributes of your rocks?" Ask them to come up with one-word descriptions of their rocks (big, small, rough, smooth, shiny, dull, heavy, light, and so forth.)

Youngsters may suggest more attributes after reading *Is It Rough? Is It Smooth? Is It Shiny?* by Tana Hoban. Some of the distinguishing characteristics they might come up with could be: size, shape, color, hardness, feel (texture), layers, shininess (luster), sharpness or smoothness (angularity, cleavage). Invite them to look in a field guide on rocks and minerals to find the terms geologists use to describe their rocks. The *Golden Guide to Rocks and Minerals* or *City Rocks, City Blocks, and the Moon* discuss what attributes geologists use to describe and group rocks. After students decide which attributes fit their samples, they could make a bar graph showing the number of rocks in their collection that they classified as hard, soft, dull, shiny, and so on.

You might ask students, "How would you figure out how hard your rock is?" An observant student who may have noticed pieces of her rock crumbling or stratching the desk or another rock, may suggest trying to stratch a hand specimen with other objects. How do geologists test for hardness? *Rock Collecting* by Roma Gans gives a brief introduction to the Moh's Hardness Scale, while a rock and mineral field guide such as *Golden Guide to Rocks and Minerals*, provides a more detailed description. The Moh's Hardness Scale measures the hardness of rocks on a scale from 1 to 10 (talc is 1; diamond is 10). Students can make their own comparisons by scratching their rocks with their fingernail (hardness 2.5), and household items such a penny (3), nail (5), glass (5.5), steel file (6), or piece of quartz (7). If the rock scratches the tool, the rock is harder.

How else can students learn about their hand specimens? You could place some hand lenses and a clear bowl of water next to the rock museum. Children may figure out on their own that these will help them see individual parts—minerals, cracks, and other features—more clearly. If a students drops his rock into a glass of vinegar, the rock will fizz if it contains organic material like shells and fossils. Geologists also use a streak plate—an unpolished piece of white porcelain—to see the distinctive colors some rocks make when you scratch them across the streak plate. Sometimes the telltale color a rock leaves on the streak plate is different from its actual color.

One way you can help students notice differences among rocks is to ask them to get to know one rock intimately. Each student, or pair of students, could be given a rock and asked to describe it in detail. They could write a poem about it, discuss what the rock reminds them of, where it might have come from, or just describe the physical attributes of the rock. The only criterion is that they have to describe it well enough for someone else in the class to pick it out from a pile of other rocks. After they are done writing, have them put their rocks together on a table and place their descriptions in a separate pile. Each student (or pair of students) selects a description that is not her own and tries to find the rock it describes. Then she places the description under the rock. After this activity is completed, read the descriptions aloud and decide as a group if they are matched correctly; then ask the authors to confirm.

Their writings may have personalized their rocks, as the authors did in *The Wretched Stone* by Chris van Allsburg, about a cursed stone, and

Sylvester and the Magic Pebble by William Steig, in which a magic pebble accidentally turns Sylvester the Donkey into a stone, to illustrate what could happen when rock collecting goes awry.

Classifying rocks by how they are made

Ask students how they would categorize their rocks based on their attributes. Would they classify them by color, hardness, texture, or other characteristic? Encourage children to come up with three to five categories and group their rocks accordingly. Geologists group rocks into three basic categories, according to how they originated: sedimentary, igneous, and metamorphic. (Later we'll see how rocks can move into different categories in the rock cycle.)

Before reading *The Magic School Bus Inside the Earth* by Joanna Cole, ask learners to be alert for the different kinds of rocks the book mentions. Afterward introduce the terms "igneous," "sedimentary," and "metamorphic." Discuss how they are formed and where they are found in or on the earth. *Sedimentary rocks* are formed in horizontal layers by the deposition of mud, sand, gravel, or rocks in valleys, river beds, and oceans. These sediments became rock when they were hardened and compacted by overlying sediments. Unlike the other two kinds of rocks, sedimentary rocks are formed at moderate temperatures at or near the earth's surface. Sand becomes sandstone, mud becomes shale, pebbles become conglomerate, and shells or lime (calcium carbonate) precipitated from seawater become limestone. You can make a sedimentary "rock" by layering different colors of PlayDoh or of plaster of paris mixed with food coloring, sand, and water into small empty milk cartons.

The origins of igneous and metamorphic rocks lie much deeper in the earth. In *How to Dig a Hole to the Other Side of the World*, Faith McNulty explores the zones of the earth and the rocks that you'd encounter if you could penetrate the crust, mantle, outer core, and inner core. Two industrious children dig a hole through different kinds of rocks, including granite, basalt, and into the material that formed them: hot, molten magma. *Igneous rocks* are literally "formed of fire." If magma cools slowly underground, as granite does, crystals of minerals have time to grow large enough to be visible to the eye. If the magma is "quenched," or cooled quickly, as when lava is forced out of a volcano, the individual crystals will be too small to see. You can grow crystals in class, some for a few days, some for a few weeks, and compare their size. *How to Make a Chemical Volcano and Other Mysterious Experiments* by Alan Kramer is a delightful book of chemistry experiments written by a thirteen-year-old boy. Among its many projects, it describes how to grow salt crystals from a supersaturated solution, as well as providing directions for two other experiments in crystallization.

Underground by David Macauley makes a nice counterpoint to *How to Dig a Hole* by describing what you would see if you dug only a *shallow* hole in the earth. Macauley's informative text and cutaway drawings show the subterranean world of conduits for water, sewage, electricity, and other services buried beneath a city.

The Magic School Bus Inside the Earth by Joanna Cole, Eyewitness *Rocks and Minerals* by R. S. Symes, and other books on rock classification explain that *metamorphic rocks* are preexisting rocks that were buried deep inside the earth and partially melted by heat and pressure. They were then transformed—metamorphosed—into different rocks. Limestone, for example, becomes marble, shale becomes slate, sandstone becomes quartzite, and granite may become gneiss. You can simulate the creation of a metamorphic rock by compressing different colors of layers of Play-Doh between two books and squeezing laterally. The layers will bend and buckle into contorted layers like the wavy bands of minerals that may be seen in gneiss or marble.

My favorite way to illustrate rock classification is with ice cream. Peel back rectangular cardboard containers of harlequin ice cream (vanilla, chocolate, and strawberry) or rainbow sherbet, fudge swirl, and chocolate chip or rocky road ice cream. Invite students to sample a sedimentary (layered), metamorphic (with wavy swirls of "minerals"), or igneous (you can see "crystals" of chocolate chips) ice cream. You might also ask the students to incorporate these textures into word pictures of sedimentary, igneous, and metamorphic rocks (i.e., sedimentary could be written using "layers" of different colors; igneous might have an image of a volcano inside it).

Have the learners return to their class collection of rocks to see how many rocks they can categorize as sedimentary, igneous, and metamorphic. There will be several "unknowns," which they may put into a fourth group. Geologists, too, find unknowns when they are exploring. They try to determine what an unknown specimen is by examining a thin slice of the rock through a microscope, performing various chemical tests, scratching it against a streak plate, comparing it to other samples found in the same area, and with other tests.

How rocks and the landscape change

How do we know that the natural landscape changes? Ask students to help you list ways that a rock or a mountain could change over time. Have youngsters analyze pictures of a young mountain and an old mountain. How are they different? Which is higher? A young mountain is taller and more jagged; an old mountain is smaller and rounder, a consequence of years of erosion and weathering.

Read *The Big Rock* by Bruce Hiscock. *The Big Rock* is the "biography" of a chunk of granite that was once part of the Adirondack Mountains. Discuss how the big rock changed through the course of its history from its creation deep inside the earth, to its burial beneath sediments in a sea. Later it was uplifted and folded into a mountain range, attacked by the elements. A million years ago, it was picked up and carried far away by a glacier, finally ending up as a glacial erratic in a forest where it will eventually wear away to sand and soil. *The Rock* by Peter Parnall continues the story of Bruce Hiscock's *The Big Rock* into modern times. It describes how animals and humans use a glacial erratic that is almost identical to the Adirondacks rock.

The Pebble in My Pocket, with its slightly different past, makes a nice comparison to *The Big Rock. The Pebble in My Pocket: A History of Our Earth* by Meredith Hooper and Chris Coady is one of the newest "rock biographies." When the story begins with a volcanic eruption 480 million years ago, nine-tenths of the earth's history has already passed. The pebble's story is an overview of geologic time and evolution, complete with a geologic timeline at the back of the book. Hy Ruchlis's *How a Rock Came to Be on a Road near a Town* is yet another "rock history" story.

What kinds of things make rocks change?

A rock can be broken down into smaller fragments in various ways, both mechanically and chemically. Ask students to brainstorm what various processes and actions can break down a rock. Their answers may include: hitting it with a hammer, rain, ice freezing and melting in cracks, wind, rivers, glaciers, plant roots growing between cracks and expanding rocks, chemical changes from acid rain, lichen, and so forth. These changes are processes called weathering (wearing away, breaking up, disintegration of a rock or soil in place) and erosion (the transportation of worn materials from one place to another).

Invite learners to go outside to look for evidence of weathering and erosion around the school yard. They might look for a stone step that is worn down in the middle from the shuffling of thousands of feet. Is there a gully under a drainspout where rushing water has excavated the soil? They should also look for hard-packed paths through the school yard where students have worn trails into the soil or grass and for other evidence of wearing down, transport, and deposition: mounds of dirt, potholes, exposed tree roots, and cracked and broken sidewalks.

After making a list of the ways that rocks break down, ask students to categorize them into physical (or chemical) breakdown. Physical breakdown would be by mechanical processes like breaking against other rocks, pounding by waves, grinding with ice, freezing and thawing, and so forth. Chemical breakdown would include acid rain, lichen dissolving rocks, and so on.

Unleash some rock destruction in class. Students might:

- Break a crumbly rock, such as sandstone or a brick, in a cloth bag with a hammer, to simulate rocks being pounded against each other by wind, waves, gravity. Even though the rock is inside a bag, students should wear protective eye gear.

- Fill a balloon with water, place it in a container of wet plaster of paris, and put it in a freezer overnight. The water inside the balloon will expand as it freezes, cracking the plaster. When water seeps into a crack in a rock, it may freeze and widen the crack: the weathering process of freezing and thawing.

- Moisten some modeling clay and shape it into two balls. Wrap them in plastic wrap. Freeze one ball overnight. After twenty-four hours, unwrap the two balls of clay and compare. The frozen one will start to show cracks. The more times you refreeze it, the larger the cracks may become. Temperatures in the mountains may drop below freezing at night but warm up during the day. This constant contraction and expansion stresses a rock, creating and enlarging cracks.

- Shake a crumbly rock or brick in a coffee can (with a tight lid) half-filled with water. Students can take turns shaking the can for a total of 1,000 times to simulate erosion by water. Have them trace the size of the rock before and after shaking.

To show chemical breakdown:

- Place a small piece of limestone or chalk in a cup of vinegar; it will fizz as it releases carbon dioxide. Acid rain dissolves limestone and marble statues.

- Remove lichen from a rock to reveal the crumbling rock underneath that is being dissolved by the chemicals in the lichen.

These activities prove that the expression, "solid as a rock," isn't all it's cracked up to be.

Glaciers

Ice is one of nature's most powerful erosive forces. Ice plucked the rock in *The Big Rock* from the mountainside and transported it many miles away. Ice has reshaped at least a third of North America as glaciers scraped, scoured, and repositioned rocks, gravel, and soil as they moved south. *Frozen Earth: Explaining the Ice Ages* by R. V. Fodor provides a scholarly explanation of the causes and effects of the Ice Age that lasted from about one million to 10,000 years ago. Although too difficult for most students to read on their own, this slim volume provides an excellent background for teachers.

Glaciers by Wendell V. Tangborn is geared for early elementary grades in that elucidating series, Let's Read-and-Find-Out Science Books. It explains that a glacier is a river of ice created when snow accumulates over a long time. When it becomes compressed into ice by overlying layers, it begins to flow. The book illustrates the areas of North America covered by the Ice Age and some of the features, like gravel pits, scratched rocks, and hills, that are remnants of the Ice Age.

You can create your own glaciers using ice cube trays or cottage cheese containers, small rocks or pebbles, and an open area of exposed soil on the playground. In the classroom, place small, angular rocks on the bottom of an empty cottage cheese cup or ice cube tray. Nearly cover the rocks with water, leaving just the tops exposed, and freeze. The next day, empty the ice from the containers onto bare soil in the school yard, so that the protruding rocks face down. Push the "glacier" across the playground to scrape and change the landscape. Bury the glacier under a thin layer of soil and let it melt to create a round depression that becomes a pond called a kettle hole.

These activities can lead into a discussion with questions like, "Are there places where there are still glaciers today? (Yes.) Are the same things happening there?" (Yes.) Geologists study modern glaciers in Canada and the Antarctic in order to try to figure out what happened a million years ago in North America from Canada to New York. *Glaciers: Ice on the Move* by Sally M. Walker provides a detailed description of glaciers and their impact today and during the Pleistocene Ice Age, the geologic period when *The Big Rock* was plucked from the Adirondacks. Walker shows examples of geologic features left by the ice on the North American landscape, including drumlins, eskers, kettle holes, glacially striated rocks, and U-shaped valleys. The extensive glossary in *Glaciers: Ice on the Move* will help anyone who is not a Pleistocene geologist.

What do rocks break into?

Ask students to recall what author Bruce Hiscock said *The Big Rock* would eventually become (sand and soil). When rocks break down mechanically, they may break into sand fragments of their component minerals. *Soil* is another end-product of the breakdown of rocks, but it has many ingredients besides rock fragments. Soil is made of plants, air, water, rocks, silt, sand, clay, all combined over hundreds or thousands of years. *A Handful of Soil* by Seymour Simon describes what's in soil.

Spark a discussion by asking, "What's the difference between sand

and soil?" After doing some firsthand investigation of soil, their answers may reflect the fact that soil is more than rock fragments: It has organic materials, both living and decaying.

Challenge students to create a recipe for soil. Place a square foot of soil on a layer of newspaper or paper towels on top of a plastic sheet (if done indoors). Students can separate the soil using tweezers, coffee stirrers, or popsicle sticks. Before they begin sorting, ask them what they expect to find in the soil and record their answers on the chalkboard.

As they pick apart the block of soil on the floor or smaller samples back at their desks, have them group similar objects together. They should put living things into a plastic jar with a lid with air holes. Some of the other things they may find: rock fragments, sand, clay, decaying leaves, roots, twigs, worms, beetles, and so on.

Look at the newspaper or paper towels under the soil. Why are they wet? (From the water in soil.) Ask students how the living creatures they find can breathe underground. (There is air in soil.)

Mix together pebbles, sand, leaves, water, twigs, and bugs in a big mixing bowl, and ask students, "Is this soil? Does it look different from your soil samples? Why?" It takes many years for the elements of soil to decay, so the missing ingredient is time. Note that there are also microbes and other decomposers in soil that are too small to see.

Together come up with a recipe for soil that includes the ingredients the young people found, as well as water, air, and time. If you could keep this soil in a garden or corner of the school yard for a year, what components might change in that time? Which ingredients would not change in a year?

Outside, compare school yard soils from different sites and depths for wetness, grain size (roll the soil between your fingers to feel its "grittiness"), compactness (try to shove a pen into the ground), components, and *porosity*. A soil percolation test compares the porosity of soil at different sites, such as hard-packed soil, clayey soil, sand, and garden soil. To perform this test, remove both ends of a large can and make a mark with a magic marker one inch from the bottom of can. Place the can into the soil to the one-inch mark. Using a graduated cylinder, pour fifty milliliters of water into the can and time how many seconds it takes for the water to disappear (or *percolate*) into the soil. To determine the rate of flow through the sample, divide the amount of percolated water by the time period in seconds, for example, 50ml/10sec=5ml/sec. Why do the rates of percolation differ? Graph the different rates. This is much like the "Perc Test" that is performed on construction sites to determine where the soil is suitable for building.

Shake different soil samples in jars of water. Observe that as they settle, different soils create layers of different colors and thicknesses. Dry the soils and then shake them through sieves to see which are finer grained.

Books that describe some of the residents of soil include *Simon Underground* by Joanna Ryder, about a mole named Simon digging tunnels to prepare for winter, *How to Eat Fried Worms* by Thomas Rockwell, about a boy who agrees to eat fifteen worms on a dare, and *Compost Critters* by Bianca Lavies. Earthworms are great soil excavators. The value of earthworms is lauded in *Worms Eat My Garbage* by Mary Appelhut, a handbook for children on how to set up an earthworm composting system. Another book, *Earthworms, Dirt, and Rotten Leaves* by Molly McLaughlin lists several experiments children can do with earthworms.

Students can observe how earthworms mix soil layers. Fill a darkened jar (wrapped in black construction paper) two-thirds full of soil. Pour a layer of sawdust followed by a layer of light-colored sand on top of the soil. Add two or three earthworms. Feed earthworms a diet of coffee grounds and crushed eggshells. After a week, remove the black construction paper and look for how the worms have carried the sand and sawdust deeper into the soil. Ask students what effect the worms have on the soil. Their burrowing turns over the soil, opening up spaces for moisture and air.

Soil takes tens or even hundreds of years to develop. It may be hard for children to visualize that the soil they scoop up in their hands may have taken many human lifetimes to form, so it may be even harder for them to grasp the vast amount of time required for most geologic processes to occur.

How Long Is Long Ago?

When students look at a solid chunk of granite, it is hard for them to believe that the rock will eventually be reduced to sand or soil. It is equally hard to believe that continents move, that limestone sea creatures can be propelled miles above the seafloor, or that coal could be compressed by heat and pressure into a precious gem. What makes all these and other geologic events possible is time—a very, very long time. Students have difficulty visualizing the concept of time, even relatively recent time. Some counting books may help children visualize big numbers, such as *Millions of Cats* by Wanda Gag and *How Much Is a Million?* and *If You Made a Million* by David Schwartz.

The frontispiece of *The Big Rock* has a pictorial representation of a Planetary Calendar. Although it is impossible to convey earth's incredibly long history of 4.6 billion years in seventeen inches, the timeline does show that animal life didn't appear until over a third of geologic time had passed, and that humans have been around for just a fraction of a moment, geologically speaking.

Some teachers make a Geologic Time Scale for the walls of their classroom or hallway on adding machine rolls or by taping together sheets of 8-1/2-by-11-inch paper, measured off by geologic periods. Other teachers make a geologic walkway down a path on the school grounds so students can literally "walk through time." *This Book Is About Time* by Marilyn Burns explains that if earth's history were a yearlong movie epic, most of the action would take place in the last three seconds, when cars, airplanes, television, space rockets, and all modern technology are invented.

Children can begin to get a sense of relative time by sequencing various objects by age. Ask students to organize objects from oldest to youngest. Include the following for them to work with: a rock, a fossil, a seashell, an old book, a photo of a student, a dinosaur model, soil, a newspaper, and a leaf. After they have arranged them in an order of their choosing, from oldest to youngest, ask them to explain their reasoning. As good geologists, if they have a reasonable explanation, that's all you can ask for. There is no "right or wrong" answer. Ask students where their objects might fit on their Geologic Time Line. The rocks and fossils may fall somewhere in the middle, but all man-made objects (and possibly the sand) would probably end up at the very edge of the paper in recent time. "Recent time" in geologic terms means the last 10,000 years.

Fossils help us read the earth's history.

You can use the Geologic Time Line to show children how long there has been life on earth. Explain that we know this from the fossil record.

Fossils

Only sedimentary rocks contain fossils, which are the tracks, impressions, traces, or preserved remains of plant and animal life. (Fossil raindrop impressions don't fit this definition, but they are a record of the past nonetheless.)

Fossils Tell of Long Ago by Aliki describes how a fish, a fern, and dinosaur footprints were preserved in stone. We learn how a woolly mammoth was frozen in ice and a mosquito was trapped for eternity in amber (common knowledge, thanks to *Jurassic Park*). Aliki explains that fossils can tell us what the past was like, "Fossils tell us there once were forests where there are now deserts. Fossils tell us there once were seas where now there are mountains." She then suggests the reader make a fossil, "Not a one-million-year-old fossil. A one-minute old fossil," by making a handprint in clay.

The class can also make fossils by mixing plaster of paris, sand, and water to make a thick paste the consistency of toothpaste. Ask children to consider what kinds of objects have the best chance of being preserved as fossils. Experiment to see what makes the best impression. Have the students coat a seashell, leaf, feather, chicken bone, or other object with petroleum jelly and set it into the plaster mixture. They can just make an impression and remove the object before it dries, or bury the fossil under more plaster of paris mixture when the first layer is almost dried. Before pouring the top layer, coat the surface where the two layers will meet with a thick layer of petroleum jelly. After both layers dry, excavate the "fossil" with lobster picks, dental tools, or other small tools.

In *If You Are a Hunter of Fossils* author Byrd Baylor and illustrator Peter Parnall create poetic images of trilobites, seed ferns, Exogyra, a curly horned seashell, ammonites, and a winged Pteranadon locked in stone. Students can use the book's many geographic references to locate where fossil-bearing rocks are concentrated, as in the gray ledges in Utah, in the side of a West Texas mountain, a Kansas wheatfield, and Pennsylvania shales. Many states have "state fossils." Children should be able to research their state fossil by contacting the state library, state archeologist, or state geologist.

No matter where you live, you can take the class on a fossil hunt. Announce that you're going to search the neighborhood for fossils, broadly defined as "evidences of the past." You are going to look for *street fossils* in mud, cement, and beach sand, such as handprints in wet cement, footprints in mud, animal tracks in snow, a date on a building cornerstone, fossils in a limestone bathroom stall, and so on. Have class members sketch or make rubbings of any street fossils they find. Ask them to try to figure out the comparative ages of their street fossils from the oldest to the youngest. Then ask them to write a class definition of a fossil.

Fossils not only tell us who was here before us, they can also sometimes tell us what they were doing, providing snippets of stories of migration, chases, battles, or parental care. Have students make a story "in the mud" using footprints of humans, squirrels, cats, dogs, pigeons, and so on. Or they might want to create a long-ago fossil picture story using dinosaur footprints.

The class could also research "living fossils" (those that have been around for millions of years, relatively unchanged, with few close, living relatives), such as the horseshoe crab, shark, and gingko tree. Try to find out why scientists think each species has managed to survive so long.

Dinosaurs

Hundreds of dinosaur books on the market feed children's insatiable appetites for these creatures. There is no more preposterous or engaging book on the subject than *Dinosaur Dances* by Jane Yolen, featuring poems about "Twinkle Toes" Triceratops, an Allosaurus hula dancer, and the disco king of dinosaurs, Tyrannosaurus rex. Much of the recent dinosaur research focuses on extrapolating dinosaur behavior, but paleontologists have yet to prove that dinosaurs square danced, waltzed, and discoed. *Dinosaur Dances* may not extend students' learning a great deal, but it is fun, as is the spooky holographic tale, *A Night in the Dinosaur Graveyard*, by A. J. Wood.

For factual information about dinosaurs, I especially like *The News About Dinosaurs* by Patricia Lauber with its authoritative illustrations by scientific illustrators and paleontologists. It presents the latest scientific thinking about dinosaurs and refutes some long-held assumptions, such as that all dinosaurs were slow, lumbering beasts; that they were cold-blooded; and that dinosaurs did not live in groups. It demonstrates how scientific theories evolve over time as new evidence arises.

As Lauber explains, scientists have studied dinosaur trackways—the fossilized impressions of dinosaur footprints—to estimate how fast dinosaurs moved and to theorize that they moved in herds. Ask a short volunteer and a tall volunteer to first walk, then run, across a field of mud or snow, or move wet feet on a sheet of paper. Compare the pace (such as the distance between the heel of the right foot and the heel of the left foot), stride (such as the distance between the impression of the right foot and the next impression of the right foot), and, if possible, the depth of the footprints. Measure and label the running footprints and walking footprints. Use these present-day footprints to come to some conclusions about analyzing dinosaur footprints. Geologists use this principle, "The present is the key to the past," to find explanations for many events they were not there to witness. Detectives call this "reconstructing the crime."

Ask students, "What parts of extinct animals are preserved?" Their answers may include bones, shells, claws, teeth, gizzard stones, skin impressions, footprints, eggs, whole insects in amber, and droppings (coprolites). The Eyewitness Book *Dinosaur* analyzes various aspects of the animals by examining their skeletal remains. An excavation activity can complement this book. Collect and clean (by boiling) an assortment of chicken bones, bury them in a box of sand, and let the students excavate them. Challenge them to try to figure out what parts of the animals the bones are. Ambitious students could even try to reconstruct the chicken. Aliki's *Digging up Dinosaurs* bolsters this activity, as it describes how a team of experts uncovers and shellacs the bones at an excavation site. Before the bones are shipped to a museum, they are photographed in place, numbered, and wrapped in tissue paper or plaster. Reassembling the bones at the museum may take many months.

Digging up Tyrannosaurux Rex by paleontologist John Horner and dinosaur fan Don Lessem (president of the Dinosaur Society and advisor for the filming of *Jurassic Park*) takes readers on a real-life dig, to excavate the largest fossil of T. rex ever found. The book illustrates how amateur naturalists contribute to science. The bones were discovered by rancher Kathy Wankel when she was out exploring the badlands of Montana. The authors detail the laborious, tedious work involved in removing such an important specimen. The find revealed that the stubby arms of the T. rex were more powerful than anyone had imagined. How did they figure that out? By the scars left on the bones in the places where the arm muscles had once been attached. By comparing the size of the arm muscles to those of other animals, they deduced that the arms of the Tyrannosaurus rex were almost ten times stronger that those of an average person.

Once they have mastered the fiercesome T. rex, students may be ready to move on to *Raptors! The Nastiest Dinosaurs*, also by Don Lessem. This book describes several species of dinosaurs, including the small, but swift Velociraptor of *Jurassic Park* fame and the giant Utahraptor, only discovered in 1991.

Students seem to have a particular talent for reciting and remembering tongue-twisting dinosaur species. In *The Magic School Bus in the Time of the Dinosaurs,* Joanna Cole transports her class to different time periods when dinosaurs existed so they can meet species that lived millions of years apart. Her students finish their unit by making a timeline with the dinosaurs placed according to their geologic time period. Her students also make up and illustrate new dinosaur names such as Bananasaurus rex and Frizzeratops. Your own students might build on what they learn about real species to create their own names.

Everybody wants to know: What happened to dinosaurs? Many dinosaur books address this question. Some suggest a cooling, changing earth; dust from long-term volcanic eruptions; or meteorites. *The Age of Dinosaurs* coloring book by Donald Glut, illustrated by Helen Driggs, not only features facts and line drawings of many different species, it offers some ideas about when and if dinosaurs died out.

Prehistoric Animals by Gail Gibbons and *Prehistoric Life* by William Lindsay continue the story past the age of dinosaurs. Gibbons's book features animals that we can recognize as earlier versions of the rhinoceros, the camel, and the shark. The Eyewitness Book *Prehistoric Life* touches on reptiles before progressing to mammals, apes, and early man. Ask students to research the early ancestors of modern-day animals like the horse, the fish, the shark, and the whale. Have them research animals living today that were around during prehistoric times (such as starfish, horseshoe crab, dragonfly, turtle, bat, opossum, crocodile, loon, and cockroach). Invite them to debate the statement, "Dinosaurs are still around today." Other aspects at the time of dinosaurs still exist today, namely earthquakes and volcanoes.

Some earth changes are rapid and catastrophic.

Earth events, such as earthquakes and volcanoes, have immediate and dramatic effects on the landscape. They are tied to the activity of plate tectonics.

According to AAAS's *Benchmarks for Science Literacy* (1993), children are intrigued by earthquakes and volcanic eruptions, but even older students are often not able to explain why they occur. Literature like *How to Dig a Hole to the Other Side of the World* can help introduce the ideas that the earth has many layers, and that its interior is very hot and molten. This can prepare the way to explain plate tectonics in more depth in later grades.

The Violent Earth

Some earth events don't happen over millions of years. Some happen with stunning suddenness and ferocity. Some Sunday newspapers carry a summary of the week's environmental disasters, such as hurricanes, earthquakes, eruptions, floods, and blizzards, in a special section called "Earthweek: A Diary of the Planet." Students might collect news reports of earthquakes, volcanic eruptions, floods, sea-level rise, meteor crashes, and other catastrophic events for their own Earth Diary.

Danger from Below and *Earthquakes,* both books on earthquakes by Seymour Simon, demonstrate how far science trade books have come graphically in the past few years. Seymour vividly describes the 1964 Alaska earthquake, "Houses began sliding apart, cracks in the pavement opened and closed like huge jaws, the ground rolled in huge waves." *Earthquakes* features a photograph of a fractured elementary school, which is sure to stimulate children's imaginations.

After reading several books on earthquakes, tell the students that they will be scripting a made-for-TV movie. Ask them to write action and dialogue for a scene for the period of time just before, during, and after the disaster strikes. They may want to include immediate aftereffects of earthquakes such as *tsunamis* (earthquake-generated sea waves), fires, and strong aftershocks. Simon's *Earthquakes* and Franklyn Branley's *Earthquakes* both suggest actions to take in case of an earthquake. *Earthquake Terror* by Peg Kehret is a novel about two heroic children on an ill-fated family camping trip on a deserted island. The parents must leave the children behind to make an emergency trip to the hospital.

Soon after, an earthquake destroys the family camper. Jonathan and his crippled sister, Abby, struggle to reach safety until they are separated by the flooding river.

Scientists are getting closer to being able to predict an earthquake using sensors that detect increasing tension along underground fault lines. But most earthquakes still occur with little or no warning.

Vulcanologists, those who study volcanoes, also use instruments that measure pressure changes inside a volcano's crater that signal an eruption may be imminent. Scientists are making strides in providing advance warnings of volcanic eruptions. In a few cases they have been able to predict them accurately enough to evacuate nearby areas safely. Even when they are expected, earthquakes and volcanoes will never be taken for granted.

Volcanoes

Volcanoes are undeniably hot topics, evidenced by the number of dramatic picture books on the subject. *Volcanoes* by Seymour Simon gives brief overviews of the eruptions of Mt. St. Helens, Surtsey, and Hawaiian volcanoes. For more in-depth accounts, see *Volcano: The Eruption and Healing of Mt. St. Helens* by Patricia Lauber. The first half of the book depicts the destruction caused by the violent explosion of Mt. St. Helens; the second half shows how much recovery of plant and animal life had taken place within a decade. *Mount St. Helens: A Sleeping Volcano Awakens* by Marian T. Place, printed a year after the 1980 eruption, has the immediacy of a news story and contains many eyewitness accounts. *Surtsey: the Newest Place on Earth* by Kathryn Lasky is a rich retelling of the birth of the island of Surtsey, off Iceland, in 1963. Surtsey and Iceland are the only parts of the Mid-Atlantic Ridge that rise above sea level.

No unit on volcanoes is complete without erupting one for the class. Bury a small, wide-necked bottle (like a baby food jar) or can inside a mountain of sand. Add four teaspoons of baking soda to the bottle. Mix together $\frac{1}{2}$ cup water, $\frac{1}{4}$ cup dishwashing liquid, $\frac{1}{4}$ cup vinegar, and a dash of red food coloring. Pour some of this mixture inside the small bottle and wait for the eruption. (If nothing happens right away, stir it up.) The baking soda and vinegar form carbon dioxide gas that mixes with the detergent to create the "lava" that bursts from the volcano like magma bubbling to the surface of the earth.

After reading several trade books on earthquakes and volcanoes, including the all-inclusive *Earthquakes and Volcanoes* by Fiona Watt, have learners mark the locations mentioned in the books on a world map. Do they make a pattern? They will see the same places mentioned repeatedly: California, Mexico City, Japan, Alaska, Chile, and Italy.

You can't discuss earthquakes or volcanoes without at least mentioning plate tectonics, the belief that the earth is divided into many plates like the pieces of a cracked eggshell that float along on a 1,800-mile-thick mantle of melted rock or magma. Some plates move up to four inches a year. Areas where the plates collide, like along the Pacific Rim, known also as the Ring of Fire, experience most of the world's earthquakes, volcanoes, and tsunamis. Where the plates are pulling apart, as along the mid-oceanic ridges, new volcanic material is being brought up from deep inside the earth to create new land. Compare a map of the plate boundaries to the map the students highlighted with earthquake and volcanic activity. They will overlap.

If you looked at a map of the continents bordering the Atlantic Ocean, you would notice that they fit together like the pieces of a giant jigsaw puzzle. This was one of the first clues that persuaded geologists that the continents may once have been joined. The supercontinent that existed 225 million years ago has been named Pangaea (generating bumper stickers that urge, "Reunite Pangaea!"). Students can piece together cutouts of the continents against the Mid-Atlantic Ridge to show how they once may have fit. (Plate tectonics is a very sophisticated concept that students may only be able to explain in high school, but you can help them begin to gather the evidence that they will resurrect to explore the topic again in later years.)

You can close the unit by asking students to brainstorm a list of natural disasters and then discussing questions like "Could these events happen in our part of the country?" "Could they have happened here long ago?" "Can they be predicted or prevented?" Then have students make up a scenario of what could happen around their locale. They may choose to make a static or interactive diorama, such as a blizzard of salt snow, a crashing tsunami drowning a plastic tub harbor, or an erupting volcano, using *How to Make a Chemical Volcano and Other Mysterious Experiments* by Alan Kramer.

Rocks and minerals impact all aspects of our lives.

From diamond engagement rings to marble bathroom stalls to the soil in our garden, rocks and their derivatives are part of our everyday experience.

The last page of *The Magic School Bus Inside the Earth* shows how rocks are used around Ms. Frizzle's school. Accompany your students on a neighborhood survey to take photos of how rocks are used in your area. Students may also choose to take photos of their residential neighborhoods or downtown area to help create a photo display for a classroom bulletin board.

Brainstorm ways people use rocks and minerals other than in building materials. Their responses may include gemstones, gold, silver for decoration or for money, petroleum products, coal for fuel, glass (from quartz sand), graphite "lead" in pencils, industrial diamonds for manufacturing, and so on. Sand itself has many uses, including in sandpaper, aquarium gravel, road beds, concrete, asphalt, sandblasting equipment, and silicon chips. Challenge them to find photographs of these in magazines to add to the bulletin board. Ask students to decide which rocks and minerals they feel are really the most valuable. Are they the ones that gleam the brightest? The ones that we use to build buildings or heat our homes? What makes one rock or mineral "precious" and another "worthless"?

Rocks and minerals are not only practical and beautiful, they are silent witnesses to the history of the earth. They teach us about events that happened long ago and give us clues to how the earth might look in the future. After we learn the language of earth science through children's literature and activities in the classroom and around the neighborhood, we can begin to be able to read the landscape ourselves like we read the pages of a book.

Children's Books Cited

ALIKI. 1988. *Digging up Dinosaurs*. New York: Harper Trophy.

———. 1990. *Fossils Tell of Long Ago*. New York: Crowell Junior Books.

ANNO, MITSUMASA. 1992. *Anno's USA*. New York: Philomel Books.

APPELHOF, MARY. 1982. *Worms Eat My Garbage*. Kalamazoo, MI: Flower Press.

BAKER, JEANNIE. 1991. *Window*. New York: Greenwillow Books.

———. 1993. *Window*. New York: Puffin Books.

BAYLOR, BYRD. 1980. *If You Are a Hunter of Fossils*. New York: Scribner Books for Young Readers.

———. 1974. *Everybody Needs a Rock*. New York: Scribner Books for Young Readers.

BRANLEY, FRANKLYN. 1990. *Earthquakes*. New York: Crowell Junior Books.

BURNS, MARILYN. 1978. *This Book Is About Time*. Boston: Little, Brown.

CHERRY, LYNNE. 1992. *A River Ran Wild: An Environmental History*. San Diego: Harcourt Brace Juvenile Books.

COLE, JOANNA. 1989. *The Magic School Bus Inside the Earth*. New York: Scholastic.

———. 1994. *The Magic School Bus in the Time of the Dinosaurs*. New York: Scholastic.

COONEY, BARBARA. 1982. *Miss Rumphius.* New York: Viking Children's Books.

FODOR, R. V. 1981. *Frozen Earth: Explaining the Ice Ages.* Springfield, NJ: Enslow Publishers.

GAG, WANDA. 1977. *Millions of Cats.* New York: Sandcastle Books.

GALLOB, EDWARD. 1973. *City Rocks, City Blocks, and the Moon.* New York: Charles Scribner's Sons.

GANS, ROMA. 1987. *Rock Collecting.* New York: Harper Trophy.

GIBBONS, GAIL. 1988. *Prehistoric Animals.* New York: Holiday House.

GLUT, DONALD. 1994. *The Age of Dinosaurs.* Philadelphia: Running Press.

GOODALL, JOHN. 1979. *The Story of an English Village.* New York: Margaret K. McElderry Books.

HISCOCK, BRUCE. 1988. *The Big Rock.* New York: Atheneum Books for Young Readers.

HOBAN, TANA. 1984. *Is It Rough? Is It Smooth? Is It Shiny?* New York: Greenwillow Books.

HOOPER, MEREDITH, and CHRIS COADY. 1996. *The Pebble in My Pocket: A History of Our Earth.* New York: Viking.

HORNER, JACK, and DON LESSEM. 1992. *Digging up Tyrannosaurus Rex.* New York: Crown Books for Young Readers.

KEHRET, PEG. 1996. *Earthquake Terror.* New York: Cobblehill Books.

KRAMER, ALAN. 1991. *How to Make a Chemical Volcano and Other Mysterious Experiments.* New York: Franklin Watts.

LASKY, KATHRYN. 1992. *Surtsey: The Newest Place on Earth.* New York: Hyperion Books for Children.

LAUBER, PATRICIA. 1989. *The News About Dinosaurs.* New York: Bradbury Press.

———. 1993. *Volcano: The Eruption and Healing of Mt. St. Helens.* New York: Aladdin Books.

LAVIES, BIANCA. 1993. *Compost Critters.* New York: Dutton Children's Books.

LESSEM, DON. 1996. *Raptors! The Nastiest Dinosaurs.* Boston: Little, Brown.

LINDSAY, WILLIAM. 1994. *Prehistoric Life.* New York: Knopf Books for Young Readers.

MACAULEY, DAVID. 1976. *Underground.* Boston: Houghton Mifflin.

McLAUGHLIN, MOLLY. 1986. *Earthworms, Dirt, and Rotten Leaves: An Exploration in Ecology.* New York: Atheneum Books for Young Readers.

McNulty, Faith. 1979. *How to Dig a Hole to the Other Side of the World.* New York: HarperCollins Children's Books.

Norman, David, and Angela Miller. 1989. *Dinosaur.* New York: Knopf Books for Young Readers.

Parnall, Peter. 1991. *The Rock.* New York: Macmillan Children's Book Group.

Place, Marian. 1981. *Mount St. Helens: A Sleeping Volcano Awakens.* New York: Dodd, Mead.

Rockwell, Thomas. 1994. *How To Eat Fried Worms.* New York: Dell Publishing Co.

Ruchlis, Hy. 1973. *How a Rock Came to Be on a Road near a Town.* New York: Walker & Company.

Ryder, Joanna. 1976. *Simon Underground.* New York: Harper & Row.

Schwartz, David. 1985. *How Much Is a Million?* New York: Lothrop, Lee & Shepard Books.

———. 1989. *If You Made a Million.* New York: Lothrop, Lee & Shepard Books.

Simon, Seymour. 1970. *A Handful of Soil.* New York: Hawthorn Books.

———. 1979. *Danger from Below.* New York: Four Winds Press.

———. 1988. *Volcanoes.* New York: Morrow Junior Books.

———. 1991. *Earthquakes.* New York: Morrow Junior Books.

Steig, William. 1969. *Sylvester and the Magic Pebble.* New York: Simon & Schuster Books for Young Readers.

Symes, R. S. 1988. *Rocks and Minerals.* New York: Knopf Books for Young Readers.

Tangborn, Wendell. 1988. *Glaciers.* New York: Harper Trophy.

van Allsburg, Chris. 1991. *The Wretched Stone.* Boston: Houghton Mifflin.

Walker, Sally. 1990. *Glaciers: Ice on the Move.* Minneapolis, MN: Carolrhoda Books.

Watt, Fiona. 1993. *Earthquakes and Volcanoes.* Tulsa, OK: Usborne.

Wood, A. J. 1994. *A Night in the Dinosaur Graveyard.* New York: HarperCollins Children's Books.

Yolen, Jane. 1990. *Dinosaur Dances.* New York: Putnam Publishing Group.

Zim, H., and P. Schaffer. 1957. *Golden Guide to Rocks and Minerals.* New York: Golden Press.

3 *Weather and Seasons*

Children, like all of us, have an abiding interest in the weather. The weather report may be the only news they listen to in order to find if a rainy forecast threatens their baseball game or if a snowstorm might cancel school. You can build on that curiosity to teach about predictable change using the wealth of books on weather and the seasons. Books allow us to observe these changes over time and to view them from a different perspective—from high above the ground, in a thundercloud, or inside a hurricane. Books on wild weather—hurricanes, tornadoes, blizzards, and the like—are sure to engage students. They are also subjects you surely would prefer to investigate through literature rather than firsthand!

Students can make firsthand observations about weather and seasons, but they need the wisdom from books to explain what is happening. Nonfiction books can help children dispel the misconceptions they often have about the origin of rain, clouds, thunder and lightning, and other natural phenomena (Miller, Steiner, and Larson 1996). Nonfiction books also suggest many simple experiments that children can do at home or in school. Fiction books, on the other hand, may help children deal with concerns they have about dangerous weather by providing role models of other children who have confronted similar fears.

A study of weather and the seasons can carry you through the school year. It also provides an excuse to get outdoors in all kinds of weather. This chapter indicates ways to use the weather and the seasons to look at the concept of changes and cycles like

- Changes in wind patterns, temperature, and moisture affect the weather.

- Weather patterns can be predicted to a degree.

- Severe weather can cause widespread destruction.

43

- The sun makes the seasons.
- Animals, plants, and humans respond to the rhythm of the seasons.
- Seasonal changes are a never-ending cycle.

Changes in wind patterns, temperature, and moisture affect the weather.

Where does weather come from? Weather is the condition of the air around us. Every time the air changes, the weather changes. The interaction of the heat from the sun, water vapor, and air combine to produce weather.

Wind and weather are caused by the unequal heating of the earth's surface. Because the sun shines most directly on the equator, the tropics receive more heat from the sun and reflect back the most heat into the atmosphere. The hot air rises and circulates away from the equator, while cool air moves away from the North and South Poles toward the equator to replace the warm air. Added to this movement is the rotation of the earth which produces the Coriolis effect of winds swirling around the earth. Water, of course, plays an important role in our weather. The heat of the sun evaporates water from the ocean and other water bodies, and currents of air distribute it around the earth.

To prove that warm air rises, clap a blackboard eraser above a lightbulb. What happens to the dust particles? Have students blow bubbles around the room and observe where the bubbles rise the most. Are they near a lightbulb, a heat register, or some other heat source? Ask students why heating vents are usually located close to the floor and air-conditioning vents near the ceiling.

Once learners have tried activities that whet their interest, reading books can introduce students to some basic concepts about the weather. As Ms. Frizzle points out in *The Magic School Bus Inside a Hurricane* by Joanna Cole, almost all our weather is created in the lower zone of our atmosphere, called the *troposphere*, from ground level to about six to eight miles above the earth. *Tropo* means *change*, and this zone is where the air and weather around us change. Shirley Cook Hatch's *Wind Is to Feel*, despite its somewhat dated look, offers a good introduction to wind, including some simple observation experiments. Another introductory book is *Feel the Wind* by Arthur Dorros.

General books on weather include Juenesse and de Bourgoing's *Weather* and Neil Ardley's *The Science Book of Weather*, which describes many experiments and plans for a weather station. Scholastic's Voyages of Discovery *Wind and Weather*, like other books in this series, features foldout and see-through pages and intriguing facts. M. Jean Craig's *Weather* offers fifty-six pages of weather facts concerning the sun and seasons, hurricanes and breezes, fog, rain, clouds, snow and other precipitation, lightning, and forecasting. *Puddle Jumpers* by Jennifer Storey Gillis describes many simple weather-related projects for kids.

Weather patterns can be predicted to some degree.

Professional meteorologists, old wives' tales, and home weather stations all help predict the weather. It can be observed and measured, yet even with computers, radar, weather satellites, and other sophisticated monitoring instruments, meteorologists can only reliably predict the weather up to a few days in advance.

Weather sayings

Before there were meteorologists, everyone was an expert on the weather. Weather lore was created to explain and predict our weather, and it was frequently accurate. Ask students to interview their friends and families to come up with a list of weather sayings. Several weather books, including Barbara Wolff's *Evening Gray, Morning Red*, describe weather lore and weather sayings. Compare these sayings to weather explanations in other books (or ask a meteorologist) to try to find out what weather conditions these folksy predictions are based upon.

> *Red sky at night, sailor's delight*
> *Red sky at morning, sailors take warning.*
>
> *When teeth and bunions ache*
> *Expect the rain to fill the lake.*
>
> *When clouds come down and turn dark gray,*
> *A rainy spell is on the way.*
>
> *If smokes goes high*
> *No rain comes by.*
> *If smoke hangs low*
> *Watch out for a blow.*

Keep a weather watch

You may want to set up a school yard weather station and have students keep a daily log of the weather. They can keep a chart with one column in which to record their weather predictions, another for recording the actual weather conditions, and a third to record the high temperature of the day.

If you want to build your own instruments for a weather station, refer to *Making and Using Your Own Weather Station* by Beulah and Harold E. Tannenbaum or to *Science Wizardry for Kids* by Margaret Kenda and Phyllis Williams. They provide directions for making weather instruments such as a barometer to measure air pressure, a hygrometer to measure relative humidity, an anemometer to measure wind speed, a rain gauge, and a wind vane.

In lieu of a hygrometer, you can use a pinecone. Avoid green pinecones and old dried-up ones. Put a pinecone outside where you can watch it open up in very dry weather and close up when it is humid.

The most basic rain gauge that meteorologists use is a tube inside a cylinder with a funnel on top. Rain falls into the funnel and flows into the tube. You can make a rain gauge using a wide-mouthed jar marked off by inches with an indelible marking pen. (Zero is at the bottom of the jar.) Set it in an open area. Measure and record the amount of each rainfall on a chart each day.

When you set up weather instruments, such as a thermometer or a barometer, place them away from trees and buildings inside a plastic milk crate turned on its side. You can lay a piece of wood weighted by a brick or rock on top of the housing to protect the thermometer from direct sunlight that would alter its readings. Professional meteorologists keep their instruments inside a ventilated shelter known as a Stevenson Screen.

To compare wind speed, have students hold a piece of string at arm's length at shoulder height and record whether it hangs down (no wind), blows straight out (strong breeze), or somewhere in between. They can make a graph that shows the angle of the string to their body.

To gauge wind direction, use a weather vane or wet your finger and hold it up in the air. The side that feels coolest is the direction from which the wind is blowing. You can also have students blow bubbles outside to determine wind direction.

Having their own weather station may motivate aspiring meterologists to read Fowler's *What's the Weather Today?* Gikofsky's *Don't Blame the Weatherman,* or Martin's *I Can Be a Weather Forecaster.*

Catch a cloud

Take students outside to look for pictures in the clouds. Have them share the images they see with a friend. They can make three-dimensional cloud pictures with cotton balls and white glue on a blue background. Their clouds could look like the actual clouds they observed, or they could make them into fanciful shapes like Eric Carle's clouds in *Little Cloud* where a cloud is transformed from a puffy cloud to a sheep, an airplane, a shark, a hat, and so on until it drifts together with other clouds and begins to rain.

Find out about different kinds of clouds, from the puffy *cumulus* (Latin for "heap") clouds in the story, to wispy *cirrus* clouds (meaning "lock of hair") made of ice crystals, to flat, layered *stratus* clouds (meaning "spread out"). Read about clouds in Tomie de Paola's *The Cloud Book,* which explains common cloud types and weather sayings, or Bruce McMillan's more authoritative *The Weather Sky.* McMillan explains which cloud types are associated with which weather fronts throughout the year. From this book, students may be able to make weather predictions by observing cloud conditions themselves. McMillan also explains why the sky is a different shade of blue on a humid summer day than on a dry autumn day, introducing the idea that even the color of the sky may vary with the seasons.

Clouds can be confusing elements of the water cycle, because many people explain them as water vapor. When you see a cloud (or fog), you actually are looking at water vapor that has condensed into water droplets. Water vapor is invisible. Clouds and fog are water in its liquid form, which is why you can see them! When many water droplets coalesce, or join together, they eventually become heavy enough to fall from the sky as rain.

Learners can measure raindrops by using a piece of cardboard, a pie plate covered with a quarter-inch layer of flour, or colored paper. At the beginning of a storm, and at ten-minute intervals, have students put a piece of paper or a pie plate in the rain for five seconds. (Use a different piece of paper or plate each time.) Have them count and record how many raindrops they capture and measure their diameter with a ruler. (Raindrops may vary from 1/100 inch up to 1/4 inch.) At each interval, students may also record the air temperature outside, the severity of the storm (light, medium, or hard rain), and whether or not the wind was blowing. You can ask learners to correlate raindrop size with how hard the rain was falling. Precipitation gets ample coverage in Jonathan D. Kahl's *Wet Weather: Rain Showers and Snowfall,* David Bennett's *Rain,* and Franklyn Branley's *Rain and Hail.*

Weather resistant

Why are boots made out of plastic and umbrellas out of nylon? Put out samples of a variety of materials—denim, nylon, Goretex®, wool, flannel, plastic, rubber, and cardboard—and have youngsters test how water resistant different materials are. Test each with a eyedropper of water to determine which materials would be best suited for rain gear. With which materials does water bead up or soak in?

Repeat the experiment on bird feathers. Read Augusta Goldin's *Ducks Don't Get Wet* to find out how waterproofing and air-filled down keeps ducks warm and dry (and helps them float).

<u>Severe weather can cause widespread devastation.</u>
Wild Weather

Wild weather such as hurricanes, tornadoes, and lightning storms can cause economic, environmental, and human hardships. Better understanding of the causes of these weather systems is leading to improvements in forecasting and tracking that allow better advance warning and preparation.

To start a unit on dramatic weather, invite a television or National Weather Service meteorologist to come to class or interview them by phone. Ask them about weather records in the state. Have students interview friends and family about any severe weather events they may have experienced, such as thunderstorms, tornadoes, hurricanes, and blizzards. Were they scared? How did they protect themselves against the storm? How long did it last? What were the aftereffects? Students can use these accounts as the basis for their own tales about wild weather and as a comparison with accounts of weather adventures they will read about in books, such as Seymour Simon's *Storms*, an introduction to thunderstorms, tornadoes, and hurricanes.

Thunderstorms

Thunderstorms typically form when a cumulus cloud begins to billow higher and higher. As the cloud thickens, the top spreads out to form an anvil shape and becomes a cumulonimbus cloud. (Nimbus clouds are storm clouds.) Strong updrafts scrape rising warm water droplets against colder, falling droplets of water or ice, making the cloud electrically charged. The electricity escapes in huge sparks or flashes of lightning. This release of energy heats up the surrounding air that then expands rapidly—creating waves of air pressure or thunder. You can create a thunderclap in the classroom by blowing up a paper bag full of air and popping it. The air escaping rapidly creates a bang.

Lightning and thunder occur almost simultaneously, but we see the lightning before we hear the thunder because light travels faster than sound. Light travels at 186,282 miles per second. Sound travels at about 1,100 feet a second, or about one mile in five seconds. To judge your distance from a lightning strike, count one thousand-one, one thousand-two, one thousand-three, and so on, from the time you see the flash to the time you hear the crash. Do this several times to see if the storm is getting closer or retreating. If it is moving closer, where is a safe place to be? Where shouldn't you be?

Books on thunderstorms, such as Stephen Kramer's comprehensive look at *Lightning*, can provide the information for students to construct a true/false safety quiz for their classmates, for example,

You would be safer standing under a grove of trees than under a single tall tree. (True)

You are safer standing under a lone tree than lying flat on the ground in a ditch. (False)

You should get out of a pool or a lake as soon as you hear thunder or see lightning. (True)

You should call your friends on the telephone during a lightning storm and talk about the weather. (False)

The only time you are safer on a motorcycle than in a car is during a lightning storm. (False)

In ancient times, Greeks and Romans believed lightning was a weapon of the gods. In some African cultures people struck by lightning had the double misfortune of being thought to be cursed. In colonial America, ringing church bells was thought to ward off lightning. Ben Franklin proved that lightning was electricity in a famous experiment in 1752. He flew a kite in a thunderstorm. Electrical charges in the atmosphere were attracted to a wire protruding from the kite. The electricity traveled to a metal key at the end of the kite where it created a spark. Franklin recognized the spark as a tiny lightning bolt. This simple but foolhardy experiment proved that lighting was electricity. (Asking students why this was not a particularly wise experiment may lead to a valuable discussion on science safety.)

Franklin also invented the Franklin Rod, which we know today as the lightning rod. A sharp metal pole projecting above a building attracts lightning bolts which are conducted harmlessly through a wire alongside the building and discharged through a metal spike buried underground.

Make a thundercloud

To simulate the electricity that eventually is released as lightning, assemble a bottle with a cork or plastic cap, a copper wire bent into the shape of a hook, a strip of aluminum foil two inches long by about one-quarter-inch wide, a comb, wool, and scraps of paper.

Make a hole in the cork or cap with an awl or wire coat hanger. Push the wire through the cap so part of it extends beyond each end. Bend the lower end into the shape of a hook. Lay the piece of aluminum foil over the hook in the wire and gently insert the cap into the bottle. Rub a comb across a wool sweater or rug to create a charge. If the comb can pick up torn scraps of paper, it is charged. Rub the comb a little more and touch the comb to the wire projecting from the bottle. The ends of the foil inside the bottle should stand apart, like a charged cloud in a thunderstorm. Students can create their own static electricity by shuffling their feet across a rug, or combing their hair to make it stand on end, or rubbing a balloon against their hair and sticking it to the ceiling.

Suggest that students interview family and friends and ask them to describe how thunderstorms make them feel. Also have them watch pets and observe their behavior during thunderstorms. Then reading about how people perceive thunderstorms will be more valuable. In *Rumble Thumble Boom!,* Anna Grossnickle Hines provides some novel explanations for thunder, such as that angels were rolling potatoes or people in heaven were bowling. In *Thunder Cake,* Patricia Polacco addresses the fear people may feel about thunderstorms. Nathaniel Tripp's *Thunderstorm!* provides a balanced view of thunderstorms from the perspectives of a farmer and his family, weather forecasters, and airplane pilots to the storm's effects on plants and animals.

Not just thunder and lightning herald an approaching thunderstorm. A rush of cold air, carried down from the thunderstorm by rain, may flow forward about three miles ahead of the storm. Thunderstorms themselves may be a prelude to harsher weather.

Twisters

In Marc Harshman's *The Storm,* a wheelchair-bound boy, home alone, withstands a tornado that destroys his family's farm. The story not only deals with the storm, describing the low wail, the green-yellow tint to the sky, the fear of the horses that precedes the tornado, but also how the disabled boy's bravery enhances his self-esteem. A book for older readers with a similar theme is Ivy Ruckman's *Night of the Twisters.* As in *The Storm,* children are on their own as a tornado approaches. As students read this novel, they may also note the warning signs before the tornado strikes. Frank L. Baum's *Wizard of Oz,* of course, is a classic tale whose plot is shaped by the onslaught of a tornado.

You can make your own twister in the classroom using a tornado tube that you can buy in toy stores or from science supply catalogs. The tube with a small opening connects two plastic soda bottles. As air and water pass each other they create a spiral that simulates the tight circulation of tornadoes, water spouts, and even hurricanes.

You might ask students to compare and contrast hurricanes and twisters. Both are created by spiraling winds, usually spinning counterclockwise in the Northern Hemisphere, they are often associated with heavy rains, and both may cause death and destruction. However, hurricanes occur over much larger areas and may last several days, while tornadoes usually last only minutes. Hurricanes usually form over warm, tropical water while tornadoes usually form over land. They both may have different names in different places: Hurricanes are known as typhoons in the western Pacific Ocean and cyclones in the Southern Hemisphere; tornadoes that form over water are called waterspouts.

Tracking hurricanes

Most hurricanes that affect the continental United States form as tropical depressions to our south. A tropical storm gains heat energy and moisture as it drifts northward over the warm waters, such as those of the Caribbean Sea or the Gulf Stream. When its sustained winds reach 74 mph, the storm is classified as a hurricane. A hurricane is fed by warm ocean waters, so once it starts to cross land, deprived of heat and energy and dragged apart by friction, the storm dissipates. You can discuss why hurricanes are most prevalent in the late summer (a hurricane is fed by warm ocean water, and the ocean is at its warmest in late summer) and early fall and why coastal cities tend to suffer the most from hurricanes. Ask students if they have ever been in a hurricane. If so, how did they prepare for it?

Tracking hurricanes by weather satellites has resulted in earlier, more accurate hurricane warnings. How satellites aid meteorologists is described in Patricia Lauber's *Seeing Earth from Space*. Weather forecasters give frequent updates on a hurricane's latitude and longitude and its chances of reaching the U. S. coast. Use a map of the Atlantic Coast to chart the changing position of a hurricane as it moves closer to landfall. Students can watch the Weather Channel for frequent updates, or if you have a ham radio, tune it to Hurricane Net 14.325 MHz Upper Side Band, which keeps track of any hurricane that threatens the continental United States or Caribbean islands.

Hurricane warnings

When a hurricane threatens, the National Weather Service in Florida issues Hurricane Advisory Bulletins about every six hours. These advisories provide updated information on the location of the storm and the wind intensity, as well as hurricane watch and warning information for the affected areas.

A hurricane watch is issued for a coastal area when there is a threat of hurricane conditions within twenty-four to thirty-six hours. A hurricane warning is issued when hurricane conditions are expected in a specified coastal area in twenty-four hours or less. Actions to protect life and property need to begin as soon as a warning is issued.

As a class, discuss what measures you would take if you were the head of Civil Defense in your area and a hurricane were bearing down on your community. Would you order an evacuation? If so, when? For what areas? Look at a road map of your comunity. Are there places, like bridges and highway tollbooths, where traffic jams are likely? How could you move people quickly away from the area? Where would you send people? What would be a safe place for an emergency shelter? (High ground, minimum of windows, strong structure, and so on.) What kind of supplies should an emergency shelter have? (Cots, drinking water, emergency lighting, radio, TV, or National Oceanic and Atmospheric Administration [NOAA] weather radio for official bulletins, food.)

As a result of this brainstorming, have children write a script for a TV or radio emergency bulletin that might include the velocity of the winds of the storm, its track, and what people should do in your area to protect themselves, their families, pets, and property. Make sure students warn residents to get to higher ground in their hurricane warning dramatizations and that they understand the most dangerous part of a hurricane is the storm surge, a great dome of water often fifty miles wide that sweeps across the coast near where the eye of a hurricane makes landfall. According to the National Oceanic and Atmospheric Administration (NOAA), nine out of ten fatalities are caused by storm surges. When the height of a storm surge is added to the normal height of a high tide and driving winds, it can create a massive storm tide that pushes water well inland and drowns coastal regions.

Theodore Taylor's *The Cay* gives a dramatic account in which a young boy, shipwrecked on a Caribbean island, survives a hurricane. Natalie Babbitt in *The Eyes of the Amaryllis* describes how a hurricane affects a family. Nonfiction books such as Franklyn Branley's *Hurricane Watch*, Norman Barrett's *Hurricanes and Tornadoes*, and Lisa deMauro's *Disasters*, also give examples of how people in various regions have weathered hurricanes.

On the lighter side, in Joanna Cole's *The Magic School Bus Inside a Hurricane*, Ms. Frizzle's students ascend in a hot air balloon and jump into storm clouds that are forming a hurricane. They are rescued by the Magic School Bus which has turned into a plane—all except the ever-unfortunate Arnold, who is eventually picked up by fishing boat.

Name that hurricane

The word *hurricane* may come from the name that the Arawak Indians of the West Indies gave their god of storms, *Huracan*. Early hurricanes had ho-hum names like Blustery, Windy, and even Dog. World War II pilots began the tradition of naming hurricanes after their girlfriends. In 1953 the U. S. Weather Bureau began issuing an annual alphabetical list of women's names for hurricanes. Since 1979, in fairness to both sexes, the list has consisted of alternating male and female names.

Have students make up their own list of names for hurricanes. They may not need to go through the entire alphabet, because on average, about six to eight hurricanes form in the North Atlantic and North Pacific each year. But be prepared! Challenge students to find out how far along in the alphabet hurricane names have reached in a single year. One book that might inform their research is *Hurricanes: Earth's Mightiest Storms* by Patricia Lauber, a fascinating book that describes some of this century's most destructive hurricanes, including Andrew, Camille, Carol, Hugo, and Iniki, a Hawaiian hurricane. Lauber contrasts how modern storm tracking by hurricane-hunting planes, radar, computer models, and satellites have prevented loss of life like when an unexpectedly powerful hurricane drowned much of the northeastern United States coast in 1938. (Much of the devastation was caused by the storm surge.) She also shares the theory that some scientists believe we are entering a period of increased hurricane activity after a relatively quiet period from 1970–1987, during which there was a major shift of our population closer to the coast.

Once students have explored wild weather conditions, they are more likely to be interested in the cyclical nature of the weather and the seasons.

The sun makes the seasons.

The Seasons

The weather changes due to the shift in the earth's tilt toward or away from the sun. The seasons are determined by changes in the amount of sunlight striking the earth, which in turn is determined by the angle of the earth's axis and the earth's rotation around the sun. The amount of sunlight increases and decreases with the seasons.

To begin a discussion of the seasons, you might put up poster paper on the four walls of the classroom with a different season printed or illustrated with an icon on each one. Ask students to go to their favorite season and write words or phrases (or paste up a collage of pictures) that explain what they like best about it. Then ask them to identify their least favorite season and describe what they don't like about it. Brainstorm a list of changes that happen over the course of a year (which might include migration, leaves changing color, buds and flowers blooming, birth, growth, snowstorms, hurricane season, vacation, holidays, birthdays, and so forth). Have children assign these changes to the appropriate season.

After these activities, you should have a fairly comprehensive overview of each season that you can build on during the unit. Rose Graydanus helps children understand the seasonal cycles in *Now I Know Changing Seasons.*

Place another sheet of poster paper next to each season and invite students to brainstorm questions they may have about aspects of each season. As they learn more about seasons, students may choose to add facts, observations, and new questions as they arise.

The Change of Seasons

Why do the seasons change? As children will discover in Franklyn Branley's *Sunshine Makes the Seasons,* it has to do with how directly the sun's rays strike the earth. The earth spins through space tilted on its axis, an imaginary line running through the poles, at an angle of about 23°. When the North Pole is tilted toward the sun, the Northern Hemisphere has its summer. That is when the sunlight strikes our region most directly.

How does the earth's tilt affect the seasons? Draw a line around the circumference of a ball (the "earth") to represent the equator. Draw another line to represents the 0 line of longitude that runs through Greenwich, England. Make an X to mark where you live on the globe. Tilt the globe on its axis at about a 23° angle (use a protractor). In a darkened room, shine a flashlight or penlight (the "sun") from a distance of six to twelve inches toward the side of the globe tilted toward it. Observe what part of the ball receives the most light. Move the flashlight to the other side of the ball so the ball tilts away from the flashlight. What part of the ball is highlighted? Gail Gibbons's *The Reasons for Seasons* illustrates the orientation of the earth to the sun at different times of the year.

Whichever half of the earth is tilted toward the sun experiences summer; the hemisphere tilted away experiences winter. *The Reasons for Seasons* offers a good explanation of how earth's relative position to the sun affects the seasons. Month-by-month natural cycles and activities for children is the approach of *Nature Through the Seasons* by Clare Walker Leslie. A cross between a story and a nature guide, *Nicky, the Nature Detective*, by Lena Anderson and Ulf Svedburg, investigates the secrets of the seasons, providing insights into how spiders spin webs, why birds migrate, why leaves change color, and other seasonal mysteries.

Animals, plants, and humans respond to the rhythm of the seasons.

Organisms have different ways of preparing for the stresses of the season, such as winter cold or summer drought. Even where the seasons are not so pronounced, animals and plants respond to changes in sunlight, temperature, and precipitation rates. Mating, birth, migration, hibernation, and other life cycle activities are tied to the changing seasons.

Animals

Animals have internal rhythms that are often triggered by changes in the seasons, which they ignore at their peril (Read Aesop's fable, "The Ant and the Grasshopper.") Diane Iverson's *Discover the Seasons* highlights animal activities for each season. In addition, she suggests seasonal recipes and craft projects. Jean Craighead George's nature series, *The Thirteen Moons*, describes the seasonal and life cycles of many different animals including alligators, chickadees, foxes, moles, mountain lions, salamanders, and deer. Bruchac and London compiled a collection of poems, illustrated by Thomas Locker, based on Native American legends, *Thirteen Moons on Turtle's Back*. Because the turtle has thirteen scales (or scutes), it is seen as a natural calendar for the year, which has thirteen moons. Like the Native Americans, early Greeks and Romans invented legends to explain the change of seasons. Have students try to track down other legends that explain the seasons.

Plants

The seasons of a two-hundred-year-old sugar maple is described in Bruce Hiscock's *The Big Tree*. It begins in the fall of 1775 with a maple seedling being buried by falling leaves and insulated by winter snow. As the young nation matures, so does the maple tree, creating a nice blend of history and natural history. Thomas Locker integrates art and science in *Sky Tree: Seeing Science Through Art* describing the seasonal changes of a tree perched on a hill by a river. *Have You Seen Trees?* by Joanne Oppenheim uses poetry and watercolor illustrations to explore leaves, fruits, and seasons. *The Seasons of Arnold's Apple Tree* by Gail Gibbons also provides inspiration for students to draw their own seasons of a tree.

One way students can examine the seasons of a tree and its whole life is by counting the rings on a "tree cookie," the cross-section of a tree trunk. Each light-/dark-ring combination represents one year of the tree's life. The wider the ring, the more favorable the growing conditions that year—ample sun, nutrients, and rain. Have students look for a narrow ring that indicates a year of poor growth and discuss things that might have slowed its growth. With hints taken from their reading, they may mention insects, lack of water, lightning, wind, fire, heavy snow, air pollution, and so forth. Sometimes you can also find evidence of damage in fire scars or indentations in the wood. Using a tree cookie or a school yard tree as a model, learners might choose to write their own biography of tree, modeled on *The Big Tree*.

Humans

Humans, too, adapt to the changing seasons with what they wear and what they do. Our bodies also respond, to a certain degree, to changes in the time of sunrise and sunset. Ask students if they wake up earlier in the summer or if they have a hard time falling asleep when it's still light outside. Students may want to keep a record of when they go to sleep and wake up throughout the year and compare it to the times of sunrise and sunset. (The results will be disrupted by the fact that students may have to wake up earlier than their body clocks want them to in order to go to school! Perhaps weekends would provide more informative results.) Ask students how their waking and sleeping schedule changes on a camping trip. In her book, *The Reasons for Seasons*, Linda Allison discusses body rhythms and internal clocks.

Leland B. Jacobs's *Just Around the Corner: Poems about the Seasons* is a collection of seasonal poems and crayon-bright paper-collage illustrations of autumn leaves, tracks in the snow, rain, and insects. Poet Myra Cohn Livingston, author of 83 books and anthologies, collaborated with Leonard Everett Fisher on poems and paintings that celebrate the seasons in A *Circle of Seasons*. These and other books of seasonal poems may inspire students to create their own compositions, such as this fourth grader's poem:

> *A winter night can be dangerous,*
> *Everyone has a great, big fuss!*
> *It doesn't matter if you're young or old,*
> *Winter nights are still frigid cold!*
> *Sometimes it gets below zero, I am told.*
> *Many, many shovels are sold.*
> *Always at the very last minute.*
> *We have shoveling races.*
> *(I always win it.)*

After you look at seasonal cycles, you might ask your students to brainstorm a list of other cycles, such as the water cycle, food webs, life cycles, tide cycles, or even wash and rinse cycles on the washing machine. This can lead to an exploration of each of the seasons and their rhythms.

Seasonal changes are a never-ending cycle.

Weather changes with the seasons. Weather and seasons have a repeating pattern year to year. There tends to be months that predictably exhibit high and low temperatures or more or less precipitation. From an early age, children recognize and look forward to predictable patterns in the changing seasons.

Fall, the Season of Preparation

Circus entrepreneur P. T. Barnum called autumn in the White Mountains of New Hampshire "the second greatest show on Earth." Frosty nights and sunny days produce spectacular fall foliage in the northeastern United States, but the fall can be glorious wherever you are, as Seymour Simon proves in his photographic journey, *Autumn Across America*. He describes autumn as "a season of memory and change." You might use that quote as a way to launch students into thinking of fall, asking, "What do you miss when autumn arrives?" and "What changes come with fall?" or "How do you know winter is coming?" Ann Schweninger's *Autumn Days*—a Let's Look at the Seasons book by Puffin Books—shows how people, plants, and animals prepare for winter.

Around September 21st, day and night are of nearly equal length around the world. This is the autumnal equinox. (The same thing happens at the spring equinox.) After the autumnal equinox, the daylight hours continue to shrink until the winter solstice when they begin to increase again. With three-dimensional, pop-up pages, *Anno's Sundial* by Anno Mitsumasa shows how the complex relationship between the sun and earth affects time. To illustrate this more clearly, have students measure the length of the shadow made by a yardstick at the same time each day (or each week). The shadow will become longer as the sun rays become less direct. When, according to students' records, is the shortest day of the year? Have students create a chart to record the change in the number of hours of daylight each day (or each week) from the autumnal equinox to the spring equinox. Record sunlight and sunset. (They can get these from the newspaper or from TV weather report if they don't want to get out of bed early.)

Ask students to make a picture book or photo album of what they do in autumn, such as rake leaves, try on last year's winter clothes, carve Halloween pumpkins, and so forth. Several picture books, including *What Happens in the Autumn?* by Suzanne Venino and *Discover the Seasons* by Diane Iverson, describe these seasonal activities.

Squirrels, chipmunks, beavers, and even woodpeckers gather supplies in preparation for the winter. Bears eat nonstop, getting ready for their winter fast. Birds and other animals migrate to warmer regions where they can rely on a constant food supply. Many plants release their seeds, and many insects lay their eggs, to ensure that another generation will emerge the next spring. Deciduous trees close down and lay off their food factories—their leaves. People harvest their gardens, add antifreeze to their cars, mount storm windows on their houses, and stack wood for their wood stoves.

How do animals prepare for winter?

What Will It Rain? by Jane Belk Moncure describes autumn from a squirrel's perspective. When a squirrel predicts that it is going to rain something just for her, various animals wish it would rain something special for them as well—cherries for a bird, cheese for a mouse, corn for a horse, and so on. The squirrel repeats every wish in sequence (good repetition for beginning readers), until standing under an old oak tree, she catches the acorns that the wind rains down. Squirrels are also featured in Roger Tabor's *Survival: Could You Be a Squirrel?* and *Raggedy Red Squirrel* by Hope Ryden, a photographic biography of mother red squirrel and her babies. *Chipmunk Song* by Joanne Ryder follows a chipmunk gathering acorns before the snow falls.

Whether you live in the country or the city, squirrels are ubiquitous, so they make handy subjects for the study of animal behavior. Ask students to keep a journal about the squirrels they see in their yards or nearby parks. Ask them to try to spend fifteen minutes watching one particular squirrel. How much time does it spend on the ground? How much time does it spend in the trees? How does a squirrel move from tree to tree? What does it gather? They may observe their squirrel collecting acorns, berries, and leaves to line its den inside a tree.

Have students observe how a squirrel uses its tail. It may use its tail for balance or as a parachute, umbrella, sunshade, blanket, or signal flag. Look for a nest of branches in the fork of a tree indicating a squirrel's sleeping spot during good weather.

Some animals cope with dwindling food supplies and worsening weather by migrating to warmer climates. One of the most wistful sights in autumn is the migration of flocks of birds heading south for the winter. Long ago, according to Roma Gans in *How Do Birds Find Their Way?*, people did not know that birds migrated. They thought they hid in holes in the ground or under the mud at the bottom of ponds all winter. Scientists have deduced that birds navigate in different ways—by the stars, the moon, the sun, the earth's magnetic field, wind direction, and landmarks such as coastline, rivers, and mountain ranges.

Migration

Migration is the act of moving from one place to another to find food or to raise young. Why do birds migrate in flocks? First, there is safety in numbers. A hungry hawk may have a hard time singling out one bird from a large flock. Each individual bird has a greater chance of survival than if it were the only one that caught the hawk's attention. Also, young birds migrating with their elders for the first time learn the route.

What triggers birds to migrate? Some studies have suggested that changes in the amount of daylight influence glands within the birds' bodies. These internal clocks alert them that it is time to leave. Other observers believe that changes in weather make birds migrate. But it is not just weather or day length that causes birds to move on; still more work needs to be done to solve the mystery of bird migration. Broaden concepts of migration by asking students to list other animals that migrate. They may cite whales, salmon, monarch butterflies, and so forth.

To further explore animals' winter behavior, notice which species of birds migrate and which remain behind for the winter. Set up a bird feeder for those who stay behind. Bird feeders filled with seeds, suet, and peanut butter can help birds survive the winter. Before adding birdseed to your feeder, have students measure the amount of seed in a measuring cup or weigh it on a small kitchen scale. Then have them do some calculations to find out how much seed the birds are eating. How much birdseed does it take to fill up the feeder? How long does it last? How much seed is used in a day, in a week? Strengthen students' math skills by having them determine how much a bag of birdseed costs. Then how much it costs to feed the birds for a week.

Instead of migrating or storing supplies for winter, some animals sleep. *Every Autumn Comes the Bear* by Jim Arnosky depicts the last few days of activity before a big bear settles into its den for the winter. As the weather cools, *Scoots, The Bog Turtle*, by Judy Cutchins and Ginny Johnston, digs beneath three feet of mud under an old willow tree to hibernate until spring.

How do trees prepare for winter?

As the days become shorter and temperatures drop, trees begin to shut down their food production. Trees need sunlight and they need moisture from the soil—both in short supply in winter—in order to photosynthesize, that is, to produce sugars from sunlight, carbon dioxide, and water. In winter trees no longer need their broad leaves to make food.

Sue Mitchell, a prekindergarten teacher whose classroom is bursting with science projects, writes the name of each of her students with indelible marker on the leaves of a maple tree outside their school. Each day the children make a check on the calendar if their leaf is still holding onto the tree. When they do fall, Sue invites the children to imagine where their leaves may have gone. Could they be floating out over the bay, piled up against a rock wall, or stuffed inside a squirrel's nest? Children may want to write a story about where their leaves might have gone. Leo Buscaglia's sensitive children's book, *The Fall of Freddie the Leaf,* may inspire some creative story ideas.

Sylvia Johnson's *How Leaves Change* and Betsy Maestro's *Why Do Leaves Change Color?* explain how bright, sunny days and cold nights help paint fall's farewell colors on deciduous trees, those trees that lose their leaves in autumn. As the tree stops making chlorophyll (the pigment that helps the plant absorb and utilize sunlight), the bright green color of the leaves fades, revealing yellow and orange pigments that had been hidden by the chlorophyll. In other trees, sugars left in the leaves are broken down by sunlight into bright red pigments.

Depending on the temperature and the amount of sunlight, tree species tend to produce characteristic fall colors. For example, *Red Leaf, Yellow Leaf* by Lois Erlert features the changes of a sugar maple tree through the seasons. Birches, aspens, and poplars turn yellow; sugar maple turns orange to red; sumac and poison ivy glow bright red; oak leaves turn brown, due to tannin, a chemical that is also found in tea and bogs. Give students sheets of yellow, orange, red, and brown colored paper and ask them to find leaves that match. Then identify the leaves using a field guide to trees. Have them trace the shape of the leaves on their colored paper, cut them out, and mount them on a tree mural.

Students can make leaf outlines by taping the backside of a leaf onto a sheet of white paper. Paint all over the edges of the leaf. Allow paint to dry and then carefully remove the leaf. Or you could help children press leaves by laying them between two sheets of waxed paper, placing a cloth on top, and ironing them. Or they may place leaves on a piece of cardboard and cover with contact paper. Another project possibility is making leaf rubbings. To do leaf rubbings, fresh leaves works best. Arrange leaves on a piece of cardboard or construction paper. Cover with tracing paper or other thin white paper. Rub the side of a crayon (without the paper sleeve) across the leaves until the outlines and veins appear.

Some trees don't change with the seasons. Conifers (cone-bearing trees) are known as evergreens because they keep their needlelike leaves in winter. Although evergreens like spruce, fir, pine, hemlock, cedar, and juniper lose some leaves throughout the year, they are never naked. According to Bruchac and London's *Thirteen Moons on a Turtle's*

Back, the trees were told that they must stay awake for seven days and nights. By the seventh night, only the cedar, pine, and spruce remained awake. Their reward was to stay green while other trees lost their leaves each fall.

Evergreens are well adapted for cold climates. Their narrow, waxy leaves retain moisture, and they contain a natural antifreeze that keeps their sap from freezing in winter. Have students compare deciduous leaves and evergreen leaves. Have them compare the texture, smell, and appearance of each. Have them rub the leaves between their fingers. Which are more durable? They may make leaf prints of each kind to use for greeting cards.

To learn more about both evergreen trees and deciduous (also called broad-leafed) trees, introduce students to Jim Arnosky's bearded woodsman Crinkleroot. A cross between Davy Crockett and an elf, this cartoon character shares a wealth of information about the structure of trees and their importance to wildlife in *Crinkleroot's Guide to Knowing the Trees.* Young naturalists can identify with Crinkleroot, who appears in a series of nature books by Arnosky. Another book by Jim Arnosky, *In the Forest: A Portfolio of Paintings,* depicts a forest through the fall and winter.

Birds, squirrels, and others, including humans, help spread seeds far and wide. Seeds have innovative designs to guarantee that they are dispersed, as Patricia Lauber illustrates in *Seeds: Pop-Stick-Glide.* Have students collect a variety of seeds and ask them to categorize them by how they think they are dispersed. For example,

- Seeds with burrs or hooks may hitchike on animal fur or people's jackets.

- Windblown seeds are light, fluffy, or shaped like helicopters or parachutes.

- Light, round seeds with corky or spongy outgrowths may float on water.

- Some plants have explosive seeds that shoot out like slingshots when bumped.

- Succulent seeds with attractive colors or smells are often eaten and passed through a bird or mammal.

Have students make a collection of seeds such as milkweed, thistle, burdock, cocklebur, dandelion, jewelweed, cranberries, apple, maple, ash, elm, and oak, and categorize them by how they travel. An intriguing variation on this is to have students make a list of all the seeds they can find in their kitchen.

Plants' production of seeds corresponds to the weather: the colder temperature and shorter day length.

Fall fog

In the fall, the air temperature can vary dramatically during a twenty-four-hour period. Have students keep a record of the highs and lows for a week and compute the differences between highs and lows and the weekly average of high and low temperatures. Because air temperature may be colder than the water, fog is a frequent occurrence in the fall (as well as in the spring when water is colder than the air). This is because water temperature changes more slowly than the temperature of the land. To prove this, put a bottle of water and a piece of black tile out in the sun. Have students record the temperature of each one. Leave them both out in the sun for several hours and record any temperature differences after every hour.

You can create a fog bank in the classroom. Fill a glass jar one-third full of water. Light a match and hold it over the jar opening. After a few seconds drop the match in the water and place a bag of ice over the opening of the jar. Hold the jar against a black background and watch a fog bank form. (The smoke provides particles for the water vapor to condense on.)

Although most weather books offer a good description of fog, fog takes on a different character in *Fog Magic* by Julie L. Sauer, an intriguing novel about a young girl who discovers a secret village that only appears in the fog. Fog is also an essential element in *Lost on a Mountain in Maine*, in which the young Donn Fendler is separated from the rest of his group when he becomes disoriented by the fog. This book is an autobiography of a boy lost for ten days on Katahdin, the northernmost mountain on the Appalachian Trail.

Winter, the Season of Waiting

Winter has been called "the season of waiting" and "the season of no motion." What is winter like where you live? Ask students to describe what winter means to them, to animals, and to plants. If you live in northern latitudes, winter probably means snow. Students there might find winter activities they can identify with in the *Six Snowy Sheep* by Judith Ross Enderle and Stephanie Gordon Tessler that relates the farcical winter sliding adventures of six uncoordinated sheep.

In the Pacific Northwest, winter is rainy and raw. In Florida, winter is the busy season, when most of the tourists visit to escape their weather and enjoy the balmy climate. Seymour Simon's *Winter Across America* compares how different regions of the country experience winter. The author takes us on a winter's journey from the Arctic Circle to the Florida Everglades. Ron Hirschi's *Winter* features few words but exquisite photographs that illustrate the season. Like Seymour Simon's books, it is one in a series of four books on the seasons.

When Will It Snow? by Bruce Hiscock captures the anticipation residents of temperate regions feel in late autumn waiting for the first snow. *Dear Rebecca, Winter Is Here* by Jean Craighead George explains the season in a novel way. In a letter to her granddaughter, the author explains the winter solstice and what happens in nature in winter. You might ask your students to use this book as a model for writing a letter describing the season to a friend who lives far away.

Let it snow! Let it snow! Let it snow!

Ezra Jack Keats's *The Snowy Day* makes children think about building snowmen and carving snow angels. *Snow, Learning for the Fun of It* by John Bianchi and Frank B. Edwards proves that snow is also good for many other uses, such as building igloos, photographing snowflakes, paving nineteenth-century highways, and staging winter Olympics. It relates facts you never knew you wanted to know, such as the biggest one-day snowfall in the United States was seventy-six inches (193 centimeters) in Silver Lake, Colorado, in 1921. Have students measure the snow depth in various places around their community, including open areas, next to buildings, and under trees. This can lead to a discussion about where snow drifts, where it melts, and why.

How much snow does it take to make an inch of water? As a rule of thumb, people figure that ten inches of snow equal one inch of rain. Have students discuss how they could find out if this is true. After each snow fall, use a ruler to measure the amount of snow collected in a large empty can or a straight-sided wastebasket. Record and graph the amount of snow that falls in each storm. Then cover the container with plastic and allow the snow to melt. Measure the amount of water left behind in a graduated measuring cup. If the students recorded the same amount of snowfall in two different storms, the amount of water they collect may differ. Why is that?

Snow geology is another topic students can study over the course of several snowfalls. Sequential snowstorms pile up layers of snow. Cut through a snowbank and you will find distinct layers almost like sedimentary rocks. When snow is partially melted, compacted, and then refreezes, it has some of the characteristics of metamorphic rock.

Students may have heard the term "a blanket of snow," but ask, "How can something so cold keep anything else warm?" In *Snow Is Falling*, Franklyn M. Branley describes, among other things, the insulating property of snow. Have students take the temperature of snow at different depths, starting at the top of a snow pile and every foot down until they reach the ground. Use masking tape to attach an outdoor thermometer to the end a long stick or broom handle and gently push it, bulb first, into the snow. Leave it in place for five minutes. Record temperatures at each level. Also take the temperature of the ground where it is not covered by snow. Where is it warmest? Why is snow a good insulator? You can explain that, like fur, snow traps a tremendous amount of air between the ice crystals.

The expression "as pure as the driven snow" used to be a compliment. Have students find out how clean snow really is by putting about a cup of snow on a paper coffee filter in a funnel and allowing it to melt through into a clean glass jar. Look at the residue left on the the filter through a magnifying glass. Compare snow samples from different locations, as near a road, under a tree, and from the school yard. Melt new snow and old snow. Where was the dirtiest snow found?

Not all the dirt in snow comes from the earth. Tiny specks of dust in the air stick to snowflakes. (Look at the sunlight streaming in through a window to see the amount of dust in the air.) Not all the pollutants in snow can be filtered out. Just as there is acid rain, there is acid snow. The students can test the pH of snow (how acid or base it is) with paper pH strips or a kit from a chemistry set or a homebrewing store. ("Normal" snow has a pH of 7).

Ask students to imagine what would happen if it never stopped snowing. We'd get a return to the ice ages as in *Glaciers*. With simple text and illustrations, author Wendell Tangborn explains where glaciers exist today and where they once existed during the ice ages. Did glaciers once cover your region? Students can refer to the map in Tangborn's book to find out.

Animals in snow

The Big Snow by Berta and Elmer Hader is a good transition book between fall and winter. It shows woodland creatures such as geese, pheasants, skunks, raccoons, among others, preparing for winter and then coping with the aftermath of the first big snow of the winter season. It answers the question, How do animals cope with the winter?

Some animals migrate. Some animals travel a few miles, as to a deer-yard, or thousands of miles, to find shelter from the weather and a constant food supply.

Some become dormant. These animals sleep a lot of the time but some may become active on mild days. Their body temperatures remain closer to normal than that of the hibernators. These include bears, chipmunks, raccoons, and snakes.

A few hibernate. A few mammals that truly hibernate are the little brown bat, the jumping mouse, and the woodchuck. More than a deep sleep, hibernation slows the heartbeat and breathing rates considerably, and body temperature drops as much as 60°F. When an animal sleeps, its metabolism slows down and its body conserves energy. During four months of hiberation, an animal may use the same amount of energy as it would in four days of activity!

Some die. Before they die, many insects lay eggs to hatch in the spring.

Some remain active. Squirrels, foxes, snowshoe hares, and other animals above and below the snow roam the wintery landscape in search of food. These are usually the creatures that are featured in trade books on winter.

Winter activities

Have students make a list of all the animals they can think of that they see around in other seasons. Categorize them by how each might deal with winter: migrate, sleep, die, or remain active. Make a mural or build a diorama that illustrates where animals are in winter. You might design your diorama so that it shows what's happening at the surface as well as underground, so your students don't forget the animals that are out of sight in winter. By cutting off one long side of a large cardboard box with a lid, like the kind copier paper comes in, you can create levels for "above ground" and "below ground."

There are many excellent books about animals that remain active in winter. Illustrations by Susan Jeffers add a magical feel to Robert Frost's poem, *Stopping by Woods on a Snowy Evening*. This book captures the animation of the winter woods that humans don't generally see, as woodland creatures peer at the bearded sleigh driver and his horse from their hiding places. In *Snow: Who's Been Here?* by Lindsay Barrett George, children follow a snow-covered trail and analyze the clues that various animals left behind. The winter forest is alive with creatures at night as *North Country Night* by Daniel San Souci and *Owl Moon* by Jane Yolen illustrate so well.

Take a walk in the winter woods and encourage students to look for signs of life such as animals tracks, scat, holes in trees, chewed twigs, tufts of fur, feathers, and rustling sounds. Who might have made them? Also, have them keep a log of the animals they see or find signs of, the date, and the location; then discuss how these animals manage to adapt to winter.

Survival is a recurring theme in many children's books about winter. In *The Moon of the Winter Bird* by Jean Craighead George, a song sparrow that normally should have migrated to Alabama with its companions stays in Ohio and becomes a "winter bird." The story describes the behavior and perils of the song sparrow. This book is part of George's series based on the sun calendar, *The Thirteen Moons*, which examines the life cycles of thirteen North American animals. In Ellen Bryan Obed's *Little Snowshoe*, a little rabbit searches the winter landscape for its mother until the mother eventually finds him. A far more resourceful animal is the *Cross-Country Cat* by Mary Calhoun. By accident, Henry the cat is left behind at the family cabin. He skis through the winter forest to rejoin his family, encountering a variety of winter prowlers along the way.

Sometimes humans intervene to help animals in need. Julie Downing's *White Snow - Blue Feather* features a child who brings bread crumbs to the birds and returns with a feather for her mother. In *Prize in the Snow* by Bill Easterling, a young boy, determined to become a hunter like the older boys, traps a rabbit, only to discover it is starving to death. Touched by the rabbit's plight, the boy leaves it the carrot he had used for bait and resolves to return again, not to trap it but to feed it. In Jan Brett's *Annie and the Wild Animals*, a small girl places corn cakes in the snow, hoping to attract a small furry animal to be her pet. Instead, she attracts a moose, a wildcat, and bear, and other assorted wild creatures. In *Deer in the Hollow* by Efner Tudor Holmes, a quiet boy named Seth communes with the animals. When he is still recovering from a serious illness, he sees two deer threatened by a vicious dog. He runs into the woods to protect them, and then collapses in the snow, too weak to struggle home. The deer lead rescuers to the boy. Although it is a heartwarming story about people and animals helping each other, it is perhaps most useful for beginning a discussion with the class about the fact that animals don't really do things for human reasons.

Besides finding food, the most important thing an animal must do in winter is stay warm. Have the class research what kind of shelters animals look for or make in winter. Then ask them to look for the best place for "their" animal to keep warm around the school building and grounds. You will need small paper cups, cardboard tops, a thermometer, a watch, and Jell-O (or another gelatin mix). Mix warm gelatin and allow it to cool to 50–59°F. Pour it into individual paper cups, one for each student, and announce that these are their animals. They must find a protected, warm spot to shelter their animal. They may choose different places: sun, shade, on a parking lot, next to a dryer vent, and so forth. After they have placed their animals, have them return in about fifteen minutes (sooner if it's a very cold day) to retrieve their "animals." If the Jell-O is still liquid, their animal survived. Repeat the activity using twice as much Jell-O. Do small animals or large ones have a harder time staying warm?

People in winter

It is not only animals that have to deal with hardships in winter. Ask students what humans have to do to survive winter. What must winter have been like for the pioneers? *Warm as Wool* by Scott Russell Sanders relates how a pioneer family struggles to survive the harsh Ohio winter. They buy some sheep, and despite losing several to poison weeds, wolves, and drowning, manage to gather wool to keep them warm over the next winter. Laura Ingalls Wilder describes how *The Long Winter* on the northwest prairie becomes almost unbearable when it snows from October to April. In Michael Emberley's *Welcome Back, Sun*, a Norwegian girl and her family live in a darkened world from September to March until the sun returns with the spring.

Some cultures are better equipped than others to deal with snow. Eskimos use snow goggles—often made from wood, bone, or ivory—to reduce the glare of the bright sun on snow. Trace the shape of the front of a pair of glasses onto cardboard, then help students cut out cardboard goggles to fit across their faces. Punch holes to attach string to tie around their heads and then cut out narrow slits where the eyes will be. The small openings perform the same function as squinting in the bright sun.

Ask your students to invent various words that describe winter after reading the *The Secret Language of Snow* by Terry Tempest Williams and Ted Major. This chapter book describes the character of snow using the vocabulary of the Inuit people of Alaska. The native people's keen observations of the winter landscape have created rich, descriptive phrases full of meaning and fascinating reading for us. The Inuits have many different words for snow, as do other native peoples.

Winter Storytime by Rita Kohn illustrates another winter pastime of Native Americans—storytelling. In the Woodland region of the Great Lakes, a grandmother explains the origin of *kokolesh*, the rabbit tail game that Native American children played indoors to help pass the time until spring.

In our culture, we tend to think of the season more in terms of winter sports than survival. People who named winter "the season of no motion" didn't have the resources we have today in these delightful winter activity books: *Exploring Winter* by Sandra Markle, *Winter Fun: A Book Full of Things to Do in Cold Weather*, edited by Laima Dingwall and Annabel

Slaight, *Exploring Nature Around the Year: Winter* by David Webster, and *Into Winter: Discovering a Season* by Nestor Williams. Each one is jam-packed with activities, projects, and winter trivia for children and classroom ideas for teachers.

Signs of Spring

The story goes that if a groundhog (woodchuck) comes out of its burrow on February 2nd and sees its shadow, it goes back to sleep for six more weeks. If it doesn't, spring is just around the corner. No one seems to know who invented this legend, but by February, we all need a little re-assurance that spring will eventually return. Help your students keep up their spirits by starting a journal of signs of spring.

Maple sugaring is a sign that spring can't be far away as cold nights and warm days start the sap flowing in the maple sugar trees. In late winter, the sap—water mixed with sugars in the tree—moves up the trunk from the roots to nourish developing buds. A small hole is drilled into the trunk and a tube is inserted into the hole to intercept the sap flow. An average-size sugar maple can yield twenty gallons of sap, enough to make one-half gallon of maple syrup. Children love to make maple taffy from maple syrup poured onto the snow. In *The Sugaring-Off Party* by Jonathan London, a child is introduced to this treat in a book sprinkled with French phrases and traditions from French Canada.

Robert Maas's *When Spring Comes*, with its photos of maple sap running, kite flying, preparing the fields for planting, and tree blossoms, can initiate a discussion about what happens in the spring, the season of re-birth. Ron Hirschi's *Spring* showcases spring in the mountains, with blooming wildflowers, a bear and cub emerging from their den, great horned owlets in the nest waiting their mother's return, robins, marmots, and a weasel changing from white to brown. An afterword describes the changes that occur in this season of new birth and new growth.

Each week, have students continue recording hopeful signs of renewal, like the ice breaking up on ponds and lakes, the appearance of insects, swelling tree buds, crocuses peaking through the snow, pussywillows, skunk cabbage, and the return of songbirds, frog choruses, and mud. Record each day's high temperature and the time of sunset. Graph these to prove that spring is just around the corner. Residents of the Moosehead Lake region in northern Maine hold a lottery each year to predict the first day of ice-out on the lake. Invite the children to challenge family and friends to predict when the ice on your local pond will break up.

Animals in spring

In Arnold Lobel's *Frog and Toad Are Friends*, a short story entitled "Spring" has Frog (the outgoing one) trying to rouse his friend, Toad, who has been asleep from November to April. Ask students to identify how these two friends realize it is spring.

Real frogs bury themselves in the mud under ponds and hibernate all winter. Warming temperatures cause them to emerge to court, mate, and lay their eggs in the water. Ask students if they have heard the frogs' croaking choruses at night. Challenge students to find masses of frog or salamander eggs to hatch into tadpoles in the classroom. Warn them to take only a few eggs and place them in a large jar of water or an aquarium. Once they hatch, add more algae and pond water to the aquarium or sprinkle a small amount of cornmeal to feed the tadpoles. Invite students to keep a journal of the tadpoles' development. After their legs appear, return the tadpoles to the pond. Bianca Lavies's *Lily Pad Pond* is a nice photo-essay about a frog.

Salamanders, toads, and frogs are amphibians. Their young live in water and after metamorphosis, move onto land, although they must stay near water to keep their skins moist and they must return to the water to lay their eggs. Books that provide background information about these creatures include *Frogs, Toads, Lizards, and Salamanders* by Nancy Winslow Parker and Joan Richards Wright, *From Tadpole to Frog* by Wendy Pfeffer, and *Frogs Are Fantastic*, with fascinating frog facts and a magnifying lens, by Robin Robbins.

Another animal that emerges from the mud in the spring is the turtle—a reptile. Ask students to research the difference between amphibians and reptiles. Reptiles have scaly skin that doesn't need to be kept moist, they lay their eggs on land, and their young breathe air. *Scoots, The Bog Turtle* by Judy Cutchins and Ginny Johnston and *Box Turtle at Long Pond* by William T. George are fact-filled biographies of turtles. Ask the children to listen to these stories as they are read aloud and list what each turtle eats, what might eat it, where it lives, and how it might protect itself. These factors and more define its *niche*, the role or position of an organism within its community. The students might want to research other kinds of turtles, such as wood turtles, snapping turtles, or the very common Eastern painted turtles, and write a story about one of them. They may want to compare land turtles to sea turtles by reading *Loggerhead Turtle: Survivor from the Sea* by Jack Denton Scott.

Students can learn about turtle anatomy by making a turtle sock puppet. Have them trace and cut out the *carapace* (top shell), the *plastron* (bottom shell), four legs ending in claws, and a tail from construction paper or felt squares. Have students study a picture of a turtle so they can draw patterns on both shells to represent the protective scales or *scutes* (which are made of the same material as our fingernails). Glue or staple the shapes to a sock, making sure that the children can fit their hand inside. Add button eyes and dots for nostrils, noting that nostrils and eyes are located near the top of the head so the turtle doesn't have to stick its head very far above water to breathe. Although they probably won't be able to illustrate this on their puppets, students should know that turtles have sharp beaks—but no teeth—to catch, hold, and slice their food. Turtles also have long necks, which students can simulate nicely with their hand inside the sock. Beside using their clawed feet for digging in the mud and tearing food apart, male turtles use their claws to tickle the chin of the female during courtship! Sea turtles don't have clawed feet; instead they have paddlelike flippers for swimming.

Spring, a time of birth

Babies are another sign of spring. Ron Hirschi's *A Time for Babies* focuses on birth. It features engaging color photos of baby animals playing, feeding, swimming, or riding on mom's back. The author points out that, although most babies are born in spring, some, such as bears, owls, and eagles, are born in late winter.

Ask students why many animals, especially in northern latitudes, are born in the spring. Their answers might reflect an awareness that spring brings warming temperatures and longer daylight. Both promote plant growth, assuring adequate food supply for animals. Milder temperatures make it easier for small bodies to stay warm, and birth early in the year allows a maximum period of growth before the harshness of winter sets in.

Putting in a garden

Spring is the time to plant your garden, even if you have to start it indoors. Encourage students to plant simple-to-grow bean seeds in egg cartons, modeled after *How a Seed Grows* by Helen J. Jordan or Gail Gibbons's *From Seed to Plant*. Have them measure their bean plant's growth each day after it breaks through the soil.

At home, students may choose to start a large vegetable garden or a window box garden, inspired by *Jack's Garden* by Henry Cole. It is a take-off on "This is the house that Jack built," adding on new phrases with each additional page. Besides showing the progress of Jack's garden, it also features around the edges of the pages close-up illustrations of insects that live in the soil, cloud types (with a professional-looking rain gauge), and various seeds and flowers.

Have students research how much room and how much sunlight each plant requires before deciding where to put their gardens. Have them measure the space, make a scale drawing of their plan, and record the cost of any seeds or plants they intend to buy. *Shaina's Garden* by Denise Lewis Patrick may make beginning gardeners feel less like novices as they are reassured by a little girl confronted with confusing expressions like "plant nursery," "vegetable beds," and "sowing seedlings." Ask the children what images these phrases conjure up for them and then what they really mean. *Spring Planting* by Rita Kohn shows how Native Americans keep rhythm with the seasons as a young girl asks Mother Earth for help in growing the seeds her aunt gave her into gourds. Lois Ehlert's *Planting a Rainbow* will inspire young gardeners with its rainbow of bright colors. This book shows how planning, planting, and harvesting a garden can keep a child busy all year long. Everything you wanted to know about gardening seems included in *Kids Garden: The Anytime, Anyplace Guide to Sowing and Growing Fun* by Avery Hart and Paul Mantel.

Spring rains

"April showers bring May flowers." Gardens need rain. So do people and wildlife, as Verna Aardema explains in *Bringing the Rain to Kapiti Plain*. After referring to some of the rain books mentioned earlier, you might want to make a rainstick as an art project. Rainsticks are used by some cultures to celebrate the rains. You will need a long cardboard tube (a wrapping paper tube works well), an awl or drywall screw, scissors or wire cutter, toothpicks, glue, dry beans, dry sand, uncooked popcorn, felt or tape, and decorative material such as wide ribbons, contact paper, or wrapping paper for decorating the outside.

Starting at one end, make a ring of small holes around the cardboard tube. Repeat this pattern every few inches until you have made holes down the entire length of the tube. Put one toothpick through two facing holes and secure with glue. After the glue dries, use wire cutters or scissors to snip off any part of the toothpicks still protruding. Close one end of the tube with felt or tape. Add dry materials. Close off other end of the tube. Decorate the outside. Turn the rainstick slowly end to end to produce the soothing rainlike sound.

Celebrating Summer

Most students aren't in school in the summer, but they can still continue their observations—at the beach, on family trips, and around their neighborhoods. Invite them to make collections of beach sand, rocks, seashells, bugs, or whatever captures their interest. Some students even document roadkills and share their findings with Dr. Splat and Dr. Squish on the Internet (roadkill@vmsvax.simmons.edu)! *Summer: Discovering the Seasons* by Louis Santrey describes many observations that children and their families can make about animals and plants in summer. Invite students to write a poem about summer before school ends, and when they return in the fall to write another using as many actual observations of the season as they can.

If they plan to travel out of state, suggest that students find out the name of the state bird and flower in each state they visit. These tell them about some of the most common or unique residents of these areas.

The summer solstice

June 21st is the first day of summer and usually the longest day of the year. It is when the earth in the northern hemisphere is tilted closest to the sun. Have them find out when sunrise and sunset is on that day. How long is daylight? At midday on this day, the sun reaches its highest position of the year. The word *solstice* comes from a Latin word meaning "sun come to a stop," because the sun seems to hang in the same spot in the sky for hours at this time of year. Invite your children to let their summer schedule "come to a stop"—to celebrate the summer solstice in a special way. In northern European countries, where the winters are long, dark, and cold, this summer festival is highlighted by all-night parties, bonfires, and torchlight parades.

Summer projects

What will they do to mark the day? Perhaps they can use the power of the sun to brew sun tea by putting several tea bags in a closed clear jar of water and leaving it in the sun for several hours. They can make sun prints using solar print paper purchased from a science museum store or hobby shop by laying flowers, leaves, or other objects on the paper and exposing them to sunlight for about five minutes. Next, remove the object and submerge the paper in water for a few minutes to make the image permanent. The paper is coated with a chemical that reacts to light. Whatever part of the paper isn't shielded from the sun by a leaf or other object will darken.

If students are looking for more projects, recommend *Exploring Summer* by Sandra Markle, which is filled with seasonal science facts, activities, and games. Or suggest they just kick back and read anything they want this summer. If they look for it, they can find science in every story!

Other Seasonal Patterns

Other places on earth also experience seasonal changes, although they may not be the seasons as we know them. Weather and seasons give us an opportunity to compare and contrast conditions in other parts of the world. Their climates are influenced by their closeness to the equator and amount of rain- or snowfall they receive.

In Ellen Kandoian's *Molly's Seasons*, a young girl in Maine wonders if the seasons are the same everywhere. With short poetic phrases and soft watercolor illustrations, Kandoian explains that winter darkness and midnight sun in summer typify far northern and southern regions, that equatorial regions have rainy and dry seasons, and that a little boy in New Zealand experiences the seasons exactly opposite to how Molly experiences them. A brief explanation of how the sun and earth's orbit determine the seasons follows the story.

There is something new to observe every day and every month throughout the year. Yet there is a constancy in the weather and the seasons that lets us predict patterns of change from year to year. We learn to recognize the signs in the clouds that indicate a change in weather; we learn to read the signs that augur the changing seasons, like bird migrations and falling leaves in autumn and swelling buds and melting snow in late winter.

There are still many mysteries surrounding the weather and the seasons, many phenomena that scientists can not fully explain, such as what happens inside a thunderstorm and how birds find their way across oceans. These are the mysteries that the young people who read about them may solve themselves someday.

Children's Books Cited

Weather

ARDLEY, NEIL. 1992. *The Science Book of Weather.* San Diego, CA: Gulliver Books.

BABBITT, NATALIE. 1977. *The Eyes of the Amaryllis.* New York: Farrar, Straus & Giroux.

BARRETT, NORMAN. 1989. *Hurricanes and Tornadoes.* New York: Franklin Watts.

BAUM, FRANK L. 1983. *Wizard of Oz.* New York: Puffin Books.

BENNETT, DAVID. 1988. *Rain.* New York: Bantam Books.

BRANLEY, FRANKLYN. 1983. *Rain and Hail.* New York: Crowell Junior Books.

———. 1987. *Hurricane Watch.* New York: Harper Trophy.

CARLE, ERIC. 1996. *Little Cloud.* New York: Philomel Books.

COLE, JOANNA. 1995. *The Magic School Bus Inside a Hurricane.* New York: Scholastic.

CRAIG, M. JEAN. 1996. *Weather.* New York: Scholastic.

DE MAURO, LISA. 1990. *Disasters.* New York: Trumpet Book Club.

DE PAOLA, TOMIE. 1975. *The Cloud Book.* New York: Holiday House.

DORROS, ARTHUR. 1989. *Feel the Wind.* New York: Crowell Junior Books.

FOWLER, ALLAN. 1991. *What's the Weather Today?* Chicago: Children's Press.

GIKOFSKY, IRV. 1992. *Don't Blame the Weatherman: Mr. G. Talks to You About the Weather.* New York: Camelot Books/Avon.

GILLIS, JENNIFER. 1996. *Puddle Jumpers.* Pownal, VT: Storey Communications.

GOLDIN, AUGUSTA. 1989. *Ducks Don't Get Wet.* New York: Harper Trophy.

HARSHMAN, MARC. 1995. *The Storm.* New York: Cobblehill Books.

HATCH, SHIRLEY COOK. 1973. *Wind Is to Feel.* New York: Coward, McCann & Geoghegan.

HINES, ANNA GROSSNICKLE. 1992. *Rumble Thumble Boom!* New York: Greenwillow Books.

JUENESSE, G., and PASCALE DE BOURGOING. 1991. *Weather.* New York: Scholastic.

KAHL, JONATHAN D. 1992. *Wet Weather: Rain Showers and Snowfall.* Minneapolis, MN: Lerner Publications.

KENDA, MARGARET, and PHYLLIS WILLIAMSON. 1992. *Science Wizardry for Kids.* Hauppage, NY: Barron's Educational Services.

KRAMER, STEPHEN. 1993. *Lightning.* Minneapolis, MN: Carolrhoda Books.

LAUBER, PATRICIA. 1990. *Seeing Earth from Space.* New York: Orchard Books.

———. 1996. *Hurricanes: Earth's Mightiest Storms.* New York: Scholastic.

MARTIN, CLAIRE. 1987. *I Can Be a Weather Forecaster.* Chicago: Children's Press.

McMILLAN, BRUCE. 1991. *The Weather Sky.* New York: Farrar, Straus & Giroux.

POLACCO, PATRICIA. 1990. *Thunder Cake.* New York: Philomel Books.

RUCKMAN, IVY. 1986. *Night of the Twisters.* New York: Harper Trophy.

SCHOLASTIC, VOYAGES OF DISCOVERY series. 1994. *Wind and Weather.* New York: Scholastic.

SIMON, SEYMOUR. 1989. *Storms.* New York: Morrow Junior Books.

TANNENBAUM, BEULAH, and HAROLD E. TANNENBAUM. 1989. *Making and Using Your Own Weather Station.* New York: Franklin Watts.

TAYLOR, THEODORE. 1976. *The Cay.* New York: Avon Flare Books.

TRIPP, NATHANIEL. 1994. *Thunderstorm!* New York: Dial Books for Young Readers.

WOLFF, BARBARA. 1976. *Evening Gray, Morning Red.* New York: Macmillan.

Seasons

AESOP. 1991. *Aesop's Fables.* New York: Gordon Press.

ALLISON, LINDA. 1975. *The Reasons for Seasons.* New York: Little, Brown.

ANDERSON, LENA, and ULF SVEDBURG. 1988. *Nicky, the Nature Detective.* New York: Farrar, Straus & Giroux.

BRANLEY, FRANKLYN. 1985. *Sunshine Makes the Seasons.* New York: Crowell Junior Books.

BRUCHAC, JOSEPH, and JONATHAN LONDON. 1992. *Thirteen Moons on Turtle's Back: A Native American Year of Moons.* New York: Philomel Books.

FOSTER, DORIS. 1973. *A Pocketful of Seasons.* New York: Lothrop, Lee & Shepard Books.

GIBBONS, GAIL. 1984. *The Seasons of Arnold's Apple Tree.* New York: Harcourt Brace Juvenile Books.

————. 1995. *The Reasons for Seasons.* New York: Holiday House.

GREYDANUS, ROSE. 1983. *Now I Know Changing Seasons.* Mahwah, NJ: Troll Associates.

HISCOCK, BRUCE. 1994. *The Big Tree.* New York: Atheneum Books for Young Readers.

IVERSON, DIANE. 1996. *Discover the Seasons.* Nevada City, CA: Dawn Publications.

JACOBS, LELAND B. 1993. *Just Around the Corner: Poems about the Seasons.* New York: Henry Holt Books for Young Readers.

KANDOIAN, ELLEN. 1992. *Molly's Seasons.* New York: Cobblehill Books.

LESLIE, CLAIRE WALKER. 1991. *Nature Through the Seasons.* New York: Greenwillow.

LIVINGSTON, MYRA COHN. 1982. *A Circle of Seasons.* New York: Holiday House.

LOCKER, THOMAS. 1995. *Sky Tree: Seeing Science Through Art.* New York: HarperCollins.

OPPENHEIM, JOANNE. 1995. *Have You Seen Trees?* New York: Scholastic.

Autumn

ANNO, MITSUMASA. 1987. *Anno's Sundial.* New York: Putnam.

ARNOSKY, JIM. 1989. *In the Forest: A Portfolio of Paintings.* New York: Lothrop, Lee & Shepard Books.

———. 1992. *Crinkleroot's Guide to Knowing the Trees.* New York: Bradbury Press.

———. 1993. *Every Autumn Comes the Bear.* New York: G.P. Putnam's Sons.

BUSCAGLIA, LEO. 1982. *The Fall of Freddie the Leaf: A Story of Life for All Ages.* New York: Henry Holt & Co.

CUTCHINS, JUDY, and GINNY JOHNSTON. 1989. *Scoots, The Bog Turtle.* New York: Atheneum Books for Young Readers.

ERLERT, LOIS. 1991. *Red Leaf, Yellow Leaf.* New York: Harcourt Brace Juvenile Books.

FENDLER, DONN. 1992. *Lost On a Mountain in Maine.* New York: Beech Tree Books.

GANS, ROMA. 1996. *How Do Birds Find Their Way?* New York: HarperCollins.

GIBBONS, GAIL. 1984. *The Seasons of Arnold's Apple Tree.* New York: Harcourt Brace Juvenile Books.

HUNKEN, JORIE. 1994. *Ecology for All Ages: Discovering Nature Through Activities for Children and Adults.* Old Saybrook, CT: Globe Pequot Press.

IVERSON, DIANE. 1996. *Discover the Seasons.* Nevada City, CA: Dawn Publications.

JOHNSON, SYLVIA. 1986. *How Leaves Change.* Minneapolis, MN: First Avenue Editions.

LAUBER, PATRICIA. 1981. *Seeds: Pop-Stick-Glide.* New York: Crown.

MAESTRO, BETSY. 1994. *Why Do Leaves Change Color?* New York: HarperCollins Children's Books.

MONCORE, JANE BELK. 1977. *What Will It Rain?* Elgin, IL: The Child's World.

RYDEN, HOPE. 1992. *Raggedy Red Squirrel.* New York: Lodestar Books.

RYDER, JOANNE. 1987. *Chipmunk Song.* New York: Lodestar Books.

SAUER, JULIE. 1986. *Fog Magic.* New York: Puffin Books.

SCHWENINGER, ANN. 1993. *Autumn Days.* New York: Puffin Books.

SIMON, SEYMOUR. 1993. *Autumn Across America.* New York: Hyperion Books for Children.

TABOR, ROGER. 1990. *Survival: Could You Be a Squirrel?* Nashville, TN: Ideals.

VENINO, SUZANNE. 1982. *What Happens in the Autumn?* Washington, DC: National Geographic Society.

Winter

BIANCHI, JOHN, and FRANK B. EDWARDS. 1992. *Snow, Learning for the Fun of It.* Newburgh, Ontario: Bungalo Books.

BRANLEY, FRANKLYN M. 1963, 1986. *Snow Is Falling.* New York: Harper Trophy.

BRETT, JAN. 1989. *Annie and the Wild Animals.* Boston: Houghton Mifflin.

CALHOUN, MARY. 1979. *Cross-Country Cat.* New York: Mulberry.

DINGWALL, LAIMA, and ANNABEL SLAIGHT, eds. 1992. *Winter Fun: A Book Full of Things to Do in Cold Weather.* Toronto, Ontario: Greey de Pencier Books.

DOWNING, JULIE. 1989. *White Snow - Blue Feather.* New York: Bradbury Press.

EASTERLING, BILL. 1994. *Prize in the Snow.* Boston: Little, Brown.

EMBERLEY, MICHAEL. 1993. *Welcome Back, Sun.* Boston: Little, Brown.

ENDERLE, JUDITH ROSS, and STEPHANIE GORDON TESSLER. 1994. *Six Snowy Sheep.* New York: Boyds Mills Press.

FROST, ROBERT. 1978. *Stopping by Woods on a Snowy Evening.* New York: Dutton Children's Books.

GEORGE, JEAN CRAIGHEAD. 1992. *The Moon of the Winter Bird.* New York: HarperCollins Children's Books.

———. 1993. *Dear Rebecca, Winter Is Here.* New York: HarperCollins Children's Books.

GEORGE, LINDSAY BARRETT. 1995. *Snow: Who's Been Here?* New York: Greenwillow Books.

HADER, BERTA, and ELMER HADER. 1976. *The Big Snow.* New York: Scholastic.

HIRSCHI, RON. 1990. *Winter.* New York: Cobblehill Books.

HISCOCK, BRUCE. 1995. *When Will It Snow?* New York: Atheneum Books for Young Readers.

HOLMES, EFNER TUDOR. 1993. *Deer in the Hollow.* New York: Philomel Books.

KEATS, EZRA JACK. 1962. *The Snowy Day.* New York: Viking Children's Books.

KOHN, RITA. 1995. *Winter Storytime.* Chicago: Children's Press.

MARKLE, SANDRA. 1984. *Exploring Winter.* New York: Atheneum Books for Young Readers.

OBED, ELLEN BRYAN. 1991. *Little Snowshoe*. St. John's, Newfoundland: Breakwater.

SAN SOUCI, DANIEL. 1990. *North Country Night*. New York: Doubleday.

SANDERS, SCOTT RUSSELL. 1992. *Warm as Wool*. New York: Bradbury Press.

SIMON, SEYMOUR. 1994. *Winter Across America*. New York: Hyperion Books for Children.

TANGBORN, WENDELL. 1988. *Glaciers*. New York: Harper Trophy.

WEBSTER, DAVID. 1989. *Exploring Nature Around the Year: Winter*. New York: Simon & Schuster Trade.

WILDER, LAURA INGALLS. 1971. *The Long Winter*. New York: Harper Trophy.

WILLIAMS, NESTOR. 1982. *Into Winter: Discovering a Season*. Boston: Houghton Mifflin.

WILLIAMS, TERENCE TEMPEST, and TED MAJOR. 1984. *The Secret Language of Snow*. San Francisco: Sierra Club Books.

YOLEN, JANE. 1987. *Owl Moon*. New York: Philomel Books.

Spring

AARDEMA, VERNA. 1981. *Bringing the Rain to Kapiti Plain*. New York: Dial Books for Young Readers.

COLE, HENRY. 1995. *Jack's Garden*. New York: Greenwillow Books.

CUTCHINS, JUDY, and GINNY JOHNSTON. 1989. *Scoots, The Bog Turtle*. New York: Atheneum Books for Young Readers.

EHLERT, LOIS. 1988. *Planting a Rainbow*. New York: Harcourt Brace & Co.

GEORGE, WILLIAM T. 1989. *Box Turtle at Long Pond*. New York: Greenwillow Books.

GIBBONS, GAIL. 1993. *From Seed to Plant*. New York: Holiday House.

HART, AVERY, and PAUL MANTEL. 1996. *Kids Garden: The Anytime, Anyplace Guide to Sowing and Growing Fun*. Charlotte, VT: Williamson Publishing.

HIRSCHI, RON. 1990. *Spring*. New York: Cobblehill Books.

———. 1993. *A Time for Babies*. New York: Cobblehill Books.

JORDAN, HELEN J. 1972. *How a Seed Grows*. New York: Crowell Junior Books.

KOHN, RITA. 1995. *Spring Planting*. Chicago: Children's Press.

LAVIES, BIANCA. 1989. *Lily Pad Pond*. New York: Dutton Children's Books.

LOBEL, ARNOLD. 1970. *Frog and Toad Are Friends.* New York: HarperCollins Children's Books.

LONDON, JONATHAN. 1994. *The Sugaring-Off Party.* New York: Dutton Children's Books.

MAAS, ROBERT. 1994. *When Spring Comes.* New York: Henry Holt Books for Young Readers.

PARKER, NANCY WINSLOW, and JOAN RICHARDS WRIGHT. 1990. *Frogs, Toads, Lizards, and Salamanders.* New York: Greenwillow Books.

PATRICK, DENISE LEWIS. 1996. *Shaina's Garden.* New York: Simon & Schuster.

PFEFFER, WENDY. 1994. *From Tadpole to Frog.* New York: HarperCollins Children's Books.

ROBBINS, ROBIN. 1996. *Frogs Are Fantastic.* New York: Reader's Digest.

SCOTT, JACK DENTON. 1974. *Loggerhead Turtle: Survivor from the Sea.* New York: GP Putnam's Sons.

Summer

MARKLE, SANDRA. 1987. *Exploring Summer: A Season of Science Activities, Puzzlers, and Games.* New York: Atheneum Books for Young Readers.

SANTREY, LOUIS. 1983. *Summer: Discovering the Seasons.* Mahwah, NJ: Troll Associates.

4 *Water from the Mountains to the Sea*

If you are looking for an ideal substance to illustrate the concept of *change*, look no farther than a drop of water. It changes from a solid to a liquid to a gas. It changes from ocean water to water vapor to cloud to raindrop in a continuous cycle. Water changes as it rushes down a mountain stream and spills into a broad river that meanders to the sea. It also changes as it moves through our bodies or through a sewage treatment plant.

While water is involved with constant change, there are some constants about water that students need to be introduced to. This unit is organized around three underlying concepts while exploring water's many changes.

All the water there is is all the water there is.

Since water covers 70 percent of the planet, the earth is aptly called the "water planet," yet even that vast amount of water is finite. Except for a small percentage that is created or destroyed in chemical reactions, the same water has existed for billions of years. The water you drink today may have been lapped up by a dinosaur millions of years ago! Although most of the earth is water, very little of it is usable by humans, land plants, and animals. Most of it is salt water (97 percent), frozen (2 percent), underground, or otherwise inaccessible to populated areas. Less than one percent is water we can use for drinking, transportation, power, industry, and recreation. Much of this fresh water is groundwater; only a fraction of it is present at any one time in lakes (0.3 percent) and rivers (0.03 percent).

You can make these statistics clearer for students by doing a simple demonstration that shows how little available fresh water there is on earth. Cut up an "apple earth." Remove one quarter—that's land. Remove almost all the remaining apple—that's frozen or salt water. The remaining sliver, too fine for us to cut by hand, is drinkable water.

Water is reused again and again.

A comment about the Hudson River helped me visualize this concept more clearly: "Between its headwaters and New York Harbor, the Hudson River passes through forty kidneys." While this statement cannot be proved, it certainly makes the point clear.

All water is connected.

Water moves all around the earth. What we do to it in one place can have far-reaching effects. As scientists and policy makers have come to realize the interconnectedness of water, educators have begun to emphasize water as a whole system. Instead of presenting discrete units that focus solely on one habitat, such as the pond or the ocean, teachers need to emphasize how all aquatic systems are interconnected through lessons on the *water cycle, watersheds,* and *water use.*

The Water Cycle

The importance of water in our lives

You might begin by asking students what they know about water by making a class list of how we use water in our daily lives. Tape the list on the wall and add to it during the unit. Several books provide a general overview that might inspire questions the class could choose to research about water. *Water, Water Everywhere* by Mark Rauzon and Cynthia Overbeck Bix incorporates short poetic phrases and color photos that capture the earth as a water planet, showing water as it changes form from water in a garden to a geyser to a cloud to snow, and as it moves over land from mountain stream to rivers to the sea. Ken Robbins's *Water*, one book in the series called The Elements from Henry Holt & Company, is a collection of hand-colored photos like an antique family album of water in its many forms. These books illustrate the many ways water has an impact on our lives and our surroundings. These books may inspire questions like:

What is water?

What are its forms?

Where does it go?

How does it shape our world (literally and figuratively)?

Where does water come from?

How does a river begin?

Another source for research questions are the "reports" written by Ms. Frizzle's class in *The Magic School Bus at the Waterworks*.

Books about water help children explore where water comes from and where it goes. They learn to appreciate the importance of clean water to them and to other communities around the world, and they learn about the inhabitants of various water systems from stream to lakes to wetlands to the sea.

Learning about the water cycle

Where does your water come from? and where does it go? are two questions that bring water directly back to students' experiences. I sometimes draw a picture of a drop of water dripping from a kitchen faucet and ask learners to help me trace the journey of the drop of water backward to its source. Then I draw pictures or symbols on the board starting from the faucet and working backward to represent such answers as pipes, pumping station, reservoir or well, rain, clouds, ocean, or lake. (*The Magic School Bus at the Waterworks* can help here.)

Then I ask, "What happens to water when it goes down the drain?" Draw students out to show that water goes through pipes to a sewage treatment plant, then into the ground, the ocean or a lake, and then it becomes clouds. Depict answers on the board to create a complete picture of a water cycle.

Several children's books depict the changes that water goes through in the water cycle. Ms. Frizzle, the adventurous science teacher in Joanna Cole's *The Magic School Bus at the Waterworks*, takes her class on a field trip in which they become part of the water cycle. After the bus rises into a cloud, the Friz threatens extra homework unless the children step outside onto the cloud. As they do, they shrink and become encased in water droplets and rain down into a mountain stream that they ride to the local sewage treatment plant.

These books also provide introductions to the water cycle: Roma Gans's *Water for Dinosaurs and You*, Sam Rosenfeld's *A Drop of Water*, and Vicki Cobb's *The Trip of a Drip*.

Classroom demonstrations

Once children have been introduced to the water cycle, several simple demonstrations can help them visualize it better. To illustrate evaporation, boil a pot of water. After a minute, hold a chilled cookie sheet over the top to act as a cold front. The evaporated water will rise and condense on the cold cookie sheet as "clouds." Turn the cookie sheet toward the students so they can see the water that has collected on it. Ask them where this water (on the metal cookie sheet) came from. Did they see the water rising? (Water vapor is invisible.) You can also show condensation by filling a Crisco can with ice, placing a glass pie plate on top of the can, and watching water from the air condense on the pie plate.

Another way to show the water cycle is to half fill a clear plastic cup with hot water. Cover with plastic wrap. Place ice cubes on top and watch "clouds and rain" form. What happened? (The warm water vapor cooled, condensed, and was pulled back down by gravity.) It may be harder to get students to realize that the water that condenses on the outside of a glass of ice water is also water vapor from the air condensing into water droplets on the cold glass. This illustrates that water vapor is in the air around us, an important concept to grasp in order to really understand the water cycle.

For another demonstration of evaporation and condensation, put water into a glass screw-top jar and secure the lid. Mark the water level with a washable felt-tip marker or grease pencil and place the jar in a sunny window. Every few days, mark the change in water level on the jar. Graph the change in water level over time. Where is the water going? Can it get out of the jar? Chill the jar and see if the water returns as a liquid. Ask students to try to figure out other ways to show evaporation and condensation, including in the weather changes going on around them.

A terrarium, another closed system, can also help illustrate the water cycle. *Transpiration*, the evaporation of water from leaves, is an important source of water to the atmosphere. A terrarium shows this vividly, but for a quicker demonstration of this principle seal a plant inside a plastic bag and place it on a window sill in the sun to achieve the same effect.

What other elements are part of the water cycle?

The water (or *hydrologic*) cycle is powered by the sun, which evaporates water from oceans, rivers, and lakes. As the water vapor rises, it cools in the upper reaches of the atmosphere and *condenses* back into liquid form. Water droplets clump together into clouds. Winds blow some of the clouds over land. When the water droplets become too heavy, they fall to earth as *precipitation*—rain, snow, or sleet.

Runoff flows over the land's surface into streams, rivers, or ponds. Water that sinks into the soil percolates through pore spaces between sand grains or through cracks in the rocks as *groundwater*. It may be stored there for a long time in underground reservoirs or *aquifers*. Water passes through many different habitats before gravity pulls it down to its lowest point, the ocean.

To sum up the water cycle, the following story, *The Biography of a Drop of Water* (reproduced with permission from the Gulf of Maine Aquarium), takes readers on the journey of a drop of water that becomes part of the water supply for the largest city in Maine. Before reading *The Biography of a Drop of Water*, suggest that students record or remember the different places that the raindrop travels in the story. Afterward perhaps students could make a mural that depicts the different parts of this water drop's journey.

One morning in Maine, a tiny drop of water squeezed out of a hole on the edge of the leaf. It hung there reflecting the early morning sun. As the air warmed, the water drop felt itself rising into the atmosphere. No longer liquid, it was transformed into invisible water vapor. The water vapor drifted upward.

Even though it was summer, the air high above the earth was cold. The water droplet condensed from vapor back to liquid again. It joined with billions of other droplets to create a cloud. A strong wind blew in other clouds until they were all bunched together like a flock of puffy sheep. After a while the clouds started jostling each other. Soon they were knocking one another about like billiard balls on a pool table. A bang of thunder announced the start of a fierce rainstorm. The water drop crashed to earth and fell into the Crooked River, which carried it, swirling and tumbling, into a large lake. The Native Americans called it Sebago Lake, meaning Big Stretch of Waters.

The water drop drifted along with the slow currents of the lake. Every year from January to April it was locked in place as ice that gleamed on the surface of the lake. Deep below, other water drops at the bottom of the lake never froze. Each spring, the water drop would cradle salamander or frog eggs. Sometimes it was swallowed by a fish and almost instantly released through its gills.

One day, nearly five years after it had arrived, the water drop was drawn into a large pipe eighty-five feet below the surface of the lake. It was swept along on a whirlwind journey that carried it twenty miles in twenty-four hours. This time it surfaced in a toilet bowl.

But its journey didn't stop there. In a swirl of flushing water the water drop was swept back down the pipe and onward to a sewage treatment plant where it was screened, disinfected, chlorinated, and inspected. Finally it was released into the ocean.

This water drop had visited the sea many times before. In fact, it had taken countless journeys that had all eventually ended in the sea. From the time the earth had formed, cooled, and created water, the water drop had been circulating through the atmosphere, across the earth or under the ground, through streams, ponds, lakes, estuaries, and oceans in an endless cycle.

Look at maps of your community, state, and region. Help students find a river that flows through their town. Trace it, possibly through several rivers and lakes, to find where it connects to the sea.

Write and/or draw a story that illustrates a raindrop's journey to the sea. Use the name of your town, a local river, and where it empties into ocean. Have students put themselves in the story. What kinds of animals will the water drop meet along the way? How will the conditions of the water change? Remind them that water exists as a solid, a liquid, and a gas, and that water may flow underground as well as across the surface in streams and rivers.

Learning about the water cycle can lead to a discussion of other cycles happening around us. You might ask learners to help make a list of cycles like day or night, the four seasons, the growth of a plant from a seed to a tree, or a frog from an egg through several stages to adulthood, the migration of whales and birds, or even the wash, rinse, and spin cycles of your washing machine. Water illustrates the environmental concepts of change and constancy; its location and form may change countless times, but it has always been conserved in some capacity since it was released from volcanic eruptions four and half billion years ago. Water recycles continuously through the states of liquid, gas, and solid. As it does, it moves around the earth. Water flows downhill, pulled by gravity, to the lowest point, the ocean, where it begins the journey again. As we said earlier, all water is connected through the water cycle, through water use and reuse, and through movement through the watershed, water flowing over and under the land to collect in water bodies that eventually all flow to the sea. This is called the *watershed*.

Watersheds

Another way to launch a discussion about water is to build a mountain of sand inside a large plastic tub. Poised with a beaker of water above the sand pile, inquire, "What will happen to the water when it is poured on top of the sand?" Some students may predict that the water will flow downhill. Another might volunteer that at least some of the water will go into the sand. If so, ask, "Where will it eventually come out?" Once you have agreed that it will come out the bottom, ask if anyone has ever watched where the water goes in a rainstorm. Some of the rainwater may collect in puddles and sink slowly into the soil or evaporate into the air after the sun comes out. In a hard rain, the water races downhill as *surface water* carving miniature river valleys as if moves across bare soil. The water that percolates into the ground becomes *groundwater* that trickles through cracks and gravel until it empties into a stream. However it travels, water eventually moves downhill, pulled by the force of gravity. The land area from which water drains into a body of water, both from above and below ground, is called its *watershed*. The watershed may cover many square miles, or it may be very small. You can trace your school yard watershed. After it rains, look for places where water is flowing or making ditches in the soil. Where does it go?

Follow the Water from Brook to Ocean by Arthur Dorros illustrates in a simple, straightforward manner how water changes as it moves through the watershed from the mountains to the sea. As the slope of the land changes, so does the speed and character of the water flowing over it. The fast-flowing water of a mountain stream can make a canoe race downhill. When a river flows across a flatter landscape, it broadens and loops back and forth across the land to find the path of least resistance. Eventually it flows out the river's mouth into the ocean. After reading this book, perhaps the children could compare the simple illustrations to streams or rivers in their communities to look for local watersheds. Look at a map of the area to try to trace a local stream back to its source and downstream to where it joins larger streams or a river or empties into the sea. Then students could find illustrations in magazines and books that show different types of streams and rivers. They can also make rivers in class by pouring water onto a stream table of sand or diatomaceous earth (obtained from swimming pool companies). Have them explain where the water goes, and how it changes but also stays the same.

The watershed in Thomas Locker's *Where the River Begins* is a rich, romantic landscape. Two children join their grandfather on a camping trip to trace the river upstream to its source—a pond in an upland meadow. At the end of the story, the boys return to their home along the river, but you are left with the desire to find out what they would discover if they followed the river in the other direction, downstream to the sea. Perhaps the students could come up with their own answers, based on their own experiences or information provided in *Follow the Water from the Brook to the Ocean*.

Another voyage to the sea is provided by Dr. Seuss, who takes us on a fanciful journey to the sea in *McElligot's Pool*. An old farmer ridicules a boy for trying to catch fish in McElligot's Pool, but the optimistic youth responds that there may be all sorts of creatures living in the Pool that have come there through watery connections with the sea. Although fantasy, the book provides a fun way to look at the concept of the continuity of water as the reader follows the water from the Pool to the sea. (You'll need to correct the misconception Dr. Seuss's illustrations imply that groundwater flows like a river beneath the land, perhaps by referring back to the pile of sand in the basin.) The students might reference Dr. Seuss's drawings of fantastic fish to invent their own images of what might live in the pool or the ocean. The book makes the important point that water moves through the watershed not only by flowing along the surface but by moving underground as well.

To further illustrate how groundwater travels, explain that it trickles through pore spaces in sand or gravel or between fractures in rocks to discharge into a spring or a stream. It can't flow like a river because there isn't enough space (except in the few places where there are limestone caves). Then put some gravel into a paper cup with holes punched through the bottom. Pour water into the cup over a catch basin. Did the water flow through the gravel? This is how groundwater moves.

It is important for students to understand that water moves downhill and that it can move through and above the earth (watershed) because water can carry pollution from a long way away (connectedness). Another book that illustrates these concepts is Schmid's *The Water's Journey*, which describes watershed and the role of the water cycle on life as the book follows water from the mountains to the sea.

Holling Clancey Holling takes us on masterful watershed journeys. *Paddle-to-the-Sea* is the name a Native American boy gives to a small wooden boat he carves before releasing the toy boat into Lake Superior. Paddle-to-the-Sea withstands a journey of several years through the Gulf of St. Lawrence and across the Atlantic Ocean. In another watershed journey by Holling, a giant snapping turtle encounters many adventures as it moves down the Mississippi River to the Gulf of Mexico in *Minn of the Mississippi*.

Students can use maps and satellite images of North America and the Atlantic Ocean to trace Paddle-to-the-Sea's and Minn's journeys. The stories are so richly detailed that students can mark specific locations on their maps, measure the distances traveled, and learn about the local culture and industries of the riverways.

You can invite students to document Paddle's journey in a timeline with events marked off by the seasons. They can also illustrate his adventures and discuss how Paddle-to-the-Sea's journey corresponds to that of water flowing down a watershed, the area of land that contributes water to a particular water body. For example, the Great Lakes watershed is the area whose rain, snow, and groundwater eventually end up in the Great Lakes.

Use Holling Clancey Holling's stories as an introduction to create a class story about how a drop of water flows from the mountains to the sea. What might happen to it along the way? What different aquatic habitats might it encounter (mountain stream, wetlands, broad river, bog, pond, estuary, ocean)? Assign student groups one of these pictures to draw:

A spring-fed mountain lake surrounded by mountains

Steep, fast-flowing stream flowing downhill with rapids and waterfalls

A river with wide, meandering course, flat floodplain along its sides

Wetlands: marsh with grasses, bog of sphagnum moss, or swamp with drowned trees

River mouth where river empties into a bay or estuary

Clouds

Rain

Ocean scene with waves and large ships

Create a picture story by having students arrange individual pictures in sequence from mountains to the sea. (There may be several different scenarios.)

Water's Journey Through Different Aquatic Habitats

After covering watersheds, you could focus on what lives in individual water systems along the watershed. Ask students, "How does water change as it moves from the mountains to the sea?"

A river begins at its *headwaters*, often in the mountains, fed by an underground spring, a mountain pond, or the runoff from rain and snow melt. Rivulets of water flow downhill, merging together to become a stream, which continues to mix with other tributaries until they all become a river flowing to the sea. Along the sides of the river, areas cut off from the main channel by a beaver dam or by a change in the river's course become plant-filled *wetlands*. The mouth of a river often opens into a broad bay or a many-fingered delta where fresh water and salt water mix. This is called an *estuary*.

The character of a stream or river changes as it progresses from its headwaters to its mouth. The steepness of the slope and the speed of the current decrease as it moves from the mountains to the plains. It changes from a narrow, straight, fast-moving stream to a slow, meandering river that curves and carves through the landscape. The water may change from clear to muddy, and from cold and rich in oxygen to warm with very little oxygen. These changes influence the type of plant and animals that can be found along the river's course.

As the waterway changes, so do the animals that can live in each section of the river. Make a mural of different aquatic habitats and predict what might live in each one. *Waters,* by Edith Chase, features paper-sculpture scenes of water from a baby brook to a smooth river getting slower and wider as it approaches the sea. Fifty-seven different animals adorn the scenes, so that students can observe what lives in each habitat. Notes at the end of the book identify a dragonfly, a snowshoe hare, a bald eagle, a cedar waxwing, and other animals that students might not have noticed or recognized as they turned the pages.

Rivers, Lakes, and Ponds

Books can help you introduce children to the different forms water takes. *Signs Along the River: Learning to Read the Natural Landscape* by Kayo Robertson depicts in pictures and brief sentences what signs of life one might find along the riverbank. It lets readers draw their own conclusions about each clue before turning to the appendix in the back of the book that explains who left these signs.

William George's Long Pond series, which includes *Beaver at Long Pond* and *Box Turtle at Long Pond,* richly illustrated by Lindsay Barrett George, depicts a day in the life of typical pond animals. Notable books about ducks include Augusta Goldin's *Ducks Don't Get Wet* and, of course, Robert McCloskey's 1941 classic, *Make Way for Ducklings.* How are animals such as beavers and ducks adapted for moving through the water? How do they keep from getting waterlogged?

Close-up color photographs of a frog make words unnecessary in Bianca Lavies's *Lily Pad Pond.* For a broader range of creatures, read Jennifer Owings Dewey's *At the Edge of the Pond.* You can also discuss what characteristics prove that a beaver is a mammal, a turtle is a reptile, a duck is a bird, and a frog is an amphibian.

Animals of the lake are featured in Ron Hirschi's *Loon Lake* and in a whimsical story of a beaver looking for a friend, by Amy MacDonald, *Little Beaver and the Echo.* Research other books that provide information about plant and animal life such as Stidworthy's *Ponds and Streams* or Parker's Eyewitness Books *Pond and River.*

Wetlands

Wetlands are worth an extended study because of their variety, their value, and their accessibility. They are found in most communities and they include freshwater marshes, bogs, swamps, and salt marshes. These are valuable nursery areas for aquatic and land animals. They absorb excess water during heavy rains or rapid snow melt and prevent flooding of the surrounding areas. They can even filter out some kinds of pollution from the water that passes through them.

Polly Brann and Susan Sedenka combine science and literature in a study of wetland habitats with their multiage primary classes at Narragansett School in Gorham, Maine, using this sequence:

1. Self-discovery, a time for students to explore learning centers with self-directed activities, reference books, storybooks, and silent reading time about ponds and wetlands.

2. Teacher-directed lessons in which the teachers lead discussions and direct experiments, explorations, and oral reading.

3. Collaborative research projects in which students create independent projects, such as animal postcards; "nature showcases" (six miniature scenes inside an egg carton each featuring aspects of an animal's or plant's life cycle, food chain, habitat, and so forth); puppets or costumes for an original play; a diorama illustrating a life cycle or habitat; a science game board; a field guide or habitat brochure; or a biography of a wetland plant or animal.

4. Presentations in which every student makes an oral report that explains how they have acquired an understanding of their subject. Before giving their presentations, teachers and students compile a list of criteria for the projects so students will have a clear understanding of what is expected of them.

Some books that describe the value of wetlands include Buck's *Wetlands: Bogs, Marshes, and Swamps* and Caitlin's *Wonders of Swamps and Marshes.* An excellent contrast to these politically correct books is *Dear Garbage Man* by Gene Zion. It's the story of a garbage man's first day on the job. Stan is very excited as he collects trash from the sidewalks of the city. At each stop he finds something too valuable to throw away: an old bed, a broken bicycle, a cracked mirror. Instead of dumping these items into the "chewer upper," he piles them on the roof of the garbage truck until it buckles under the load. Stan invites the neighbors to help themselves, which they do with a shout. A great recycling story? It would have been if it had ended there. Instead, Stan returns the next morning to find all the junk again piled along his route, rejected by their finders. But he brightens as a new thought occurs to him: "All this stuff will fill in lots and lots of swamps!" to create new parks and playgrounds. When looking at the copyright, I discovered it was originally written in 1957 (but reprinted in 1988) when we believed wetlands were wastelands, best served by filling them in to make "useful" land. Although not intentionally as *A River Ran Wild* does, *Dear Garbage Man* illustrates how far our collective environmental consciousness has been raised.

Bogs

Bogs are stagnant wetlands, often completely covered by a floating mat of sphagnum moss. When the moss dies, it decays slowly, making the tea-colored water as acid as orange juice. Sphagnum moss (also called peat moss) is so absorbent that it was used by Native Americans for diapers and in World War I field hospitals for dressing wounds. It is also a smoky, cheap fuel in places like Ireland and Scandinavia. In fact, peat diggers have made unsettling discoveries when they were extracting peat from bogs. They unearthed perfectly preserved human bodies. Thinking they were recent murder victims, they called in the police and eventually learned the bodies were fifteen hundred to two thousand years old, probably sacrifices to the gods. P. V. Glob's *The Bog People* and Charlotte Wilcox's *Mummies and Their Mysteries* describe these fascinating bog people unearthed from northern European bogs.

Bogs are also home to carniverous pitcher plants, Venus-flytraps, and sundews that compensate for the lack of nutrients in the acid habitat by eating insects. These insect eaters can create a dramatic terrarium scene. Jerome Wexler's *Sundew Stranglers: Plants That Eat Insects* shows close-up color photos of a wide variety of carniverous plants, including the Venus-flytrap, butterwort, rainbow plant, pitcher plant, and especially sundews. It was Charles Darwin who discovered the secret of the sundew 120 years ago, after observing how proteins (as in insects) stimulate the sticky leaves to grow and curl around the victim. Photos in the book illustrate how the protein in egg white triggers the growth of sundew leaves over several hours.

Challenge students to draw or model a plant that can catch insects. It must have a way to attract, catch, and hold an insect. Point out the shiny, sticky droplets on the surface of the sundew, or the bright red veins on the vase-shaped pitcher plant complete with a convenient landing pad and downward pointing hairs, or the trigger hairs of the Venus-flytrap that cause the trap to close when an insect's feet tickles them.

Although few fish thrive there, a bog can support turtles, frogs, insects, and birds. *Scoots, The Bog Turtle* weaves the natural history of the bog turtle into an engaging wildlife biography. *Mystery of the Bog Forest*, by longtime nature writers Lorus J. Milne and Margery Milne, provides in-depth information about the ecology of bogs in chapter form with black-and-white photos. Do your students know where cranberries come from? *Cranberries: Fruit of the Bogs* by Diane Burns explains the history, distribution, cultivation, and harvesting of the bright red berries.

Estuaries

The most significant difference between a mountain stream and the ocean is the change in salinity. Ask students if they have swum in a lake and in the ocean. In which one is it easier to float? The salt in the ocean makes the water denser so it can support heavier objects.

Provide a large pan of fresh, warm water, a container of salt, and small objects that may or may not float, such as cork, plastic, hard-boiled eggs, fruits and vegetables, nuts, wood, and metal. Encourage students to predict which objects will float, then have them try to float various objects in a bowl of fresh water. Ask them to separate objects as they are tested into two groups: those that float in fresh water and those that do not. Then let students add as much salt to the water as stirring will dissolve. Try floating the objects that sank in the fresh water. Do any more float now? Ask what would happen if we put a gold-fish in the salty water now. You might need to point out that most animals can live *either* in fresh water or in salt water, but not in both.

Now show students a container of fresh water. Add about a tea-spoon of salt. This type of water is not as fresh as pond water or drinking water or as salty as the sea. It is something in between—an estuary. An estuary is a protected place where the river meets the sea. Estuaries were often overlooked in the past as subjects for study by researchers and by teachers. People now recognize that estuaries, the protected bays or harbors where rivers meet the sea, are important nurseries and feeding areas for sea creatures. They can also provide flood control for surrounding areas and can even filter out pollution to some degree.

If you live near the coast, collect one cup of pond water, one cup of water from an estuary, and one from the ocean. Put each sample into a separate pie plate and allow the water to evaporate. What is left behind? Which sample contains the most salt? Which have mud or fine sediments?

Until recently, few children's books dealt with estuaries. *Estuaries: Where Rivers Meet the Sea*, by Laurence Pringle, written in 1973, was the definitive work. Now stories about estuarine life such as *The Day They Left the Bay, Sid and Sal's Famous Channel Marker Diner*, and *Chadwick the Crab* provide delightful introductions to this habitat.

Estuaries are described variously as bays, sloughs, deltas, and salt marshes and comprise a large part of the coastline. To help students get an idea of how extensive estuaries are have them look at a map of the United States. Wherever a river empties into the ocean, chances are it is an estuary. Notice how many large cities are built next to (or on) estuaries (San Franciso, Boston, New York, to name a few). These locations offered the best of both worlds—access to fish and other fruits of the sea as well as to fresh water and interior transportation routes via the rivers.

Estuaries also have interesting residents such as the horseshoe crab, a prehistoric animal whose closest living relatives are spiders and scorpions. With ten eyes, a spiny tail, and an armored shell, this creature is as fascinating as the dinosaurs with whom its ancestors coexisted. Nancy Day's *The Horseshoe Crab*, John Waters's *The Crab from Yesterday*, and Suzanne Tate's *Harry Horseshoe Crab: A Tale of Crawly Creatures* are my favorites among the children's books on horseshoe crabs. John Waters's book, *The Crab from Yesterday*, has a sensitive environmental theme as it documents the practice of offering a bounty on horseshoe crabs. Clammers believed these mud muckers devoured baby seed clams, thus threatening their livelihoods. This is a tale of a young boy who receives a few pennies for a huge horseshoe crab he picks up from the beach where she has just laid her eggs. The animal, along with dozens of others, is dragged to the dump to die. When the boy encounters her again on his way home, he regrets his act and returns her to the bay, dropping the pennies into the water one by one after her. Suzanne Tate's *Harry Horseshoe Crab*, written for very young children, nevertheless accurately describes the practice of extracting horeseshoe-crab blood, which is used to diagnose human diseases such as spinal meningitis. (The blood donor is released unharmed.)

The horseshoe crab is an excellent example of an animal once considered a pest that is now highly valued for its benefits to humanity. Perhaps the students can brainstorm a list of other animals that are "unloved" by humans. Why do we dislike or fear them? Might they have some value now or in the future? (For example, shark cartilage may someday help cure cancer.)

Other estuary creatures are featured in Suzanne Tate's Nature Series for beginning readers, including *Pearlie Oyster, Flossie Flounder, Sammy Shrimp, Mary Manatee, Crabby and Nabby: A Tale of Two Blue Crabs*, and more. Jane Weinberger's *Cory the Cormorant* and Margaret Lane's *The Fish: Story of the Stickleback* are also informative, enjoyable books about estuary visitors.

Class demonstrations

An easy activity—*Mystery Solutions*—using water and salt illustrates the differences between fresh water, brackish water (in estuaries), and salt water. Provide each group of students with three clear plastic glasses of water into which you have already added three different food colorings and amounts of salt:

the first glass (green) has *no* salt

the second glass (red) has *two* teaspoons of salt

the third glass (blue) has *four* teaspoons of salt

The order of the glasses should be mixed up when they are presented to students.

Each team of students should have three colored solutions, a clear plastic straw marked with three lines one centimeter apart, crayons matching the colored solutions, an empty cup for waste water, and paper to record attempts. A team member holds an index finger over the top of the straw and holds the straw vertically as he places it into one solution up to the first centimeter mark. Have him lift the finger briefly and then put his finger back over the straw before lifting it out of the water. Have him repeat with each solution, filling to each line until the student has tried all liquids. Students should keep track of the sequences they have tried by marking a paper with the corresponding colors of crayons.

Students should keep trying different sequences until they find an arrangement in which all three colors are distinctly layered in the straw. Because the correct sequence creates well-defined layers, students instantly recognize when they have found the correct sequence as the lighter, less saline water floats on the denser, saltier water. Fresh water floats on the saltier estuarine water which, in turn, floats on the saltiest layer, the ocean water.

Living in two worlds

Ask students to predict what would happen if you put a goldfish into the estuary or ocean. Most aquatic animals can only live in fresh water or in salt water. There are animals that bridge both worlds: *anadromous* fishes like salmon that live in salt water and spawn in freshwater streams and *catadromous* eels that live in fresh water and spawn in the Sargasso Sea.

Come Back, Salmon by Molly Cone is the account of fifth-grade students who adopted Pigeon Creek in Washington state. They inspired the community to clean up the stream where salmon once spawned. The children hatched salmon eggs in their classroom and raised the fry until they were large enough to release into the creek. The children were worried that the salmon might not come back, but they did!

Even though these students raised Pacific salmon, Bianca Lavies's *The Atlantic Salmon* complements their project as its close-up photographs document the passages of a salmon's life from egg to adulthood. In an afterword, Lavies explains the challenges she encountered

trying to photograph Atlantic salmon in the wild. Like *Paddle-to-the-Sea*, salmon undertake long journeys that take them from fresh to salt water. Find out from local anglers whether salmon are found in your area. Were they once common before dams and pollution blocked their way?

Read books and interview fisheries biologists, such as fish hatchery operators, wildlife wardens, or anglers to research the obstacles and aids that salmon encounter when they travel from their mountain stream to spend a year or more in the ocean before returning to their birthplace. Some of the possible obstacles include: dams, pollution, predators, fishermen, fishing gear, waterfalls, disease, chemicals in the water that mask the smell of their home stream, and so on. Some possible aids could be scientists curing salmon diseases, fish farming that raises salmon in protected pens, conservation laws, fish ladders to lift salmon over dams, clean water, swift currents, and so forth. Use this list to create a board game (or a maze) that incorporates these obstacles and aids to move the salmon game pieces backward or forward on the game board.

Water Use

As water passes through many habitats, it is used by plants, animals, and humans along the way. All living things need water. Organisms crowd the water's edge, drawn by its life-giving properties. Plants grow lushly along a stream bank or flood plain. Animals flock to an African waterhole. Humans build their towns and cities along waterways and venture into uncharted territory following the river's path. We use water for transportation, food, drinking, washing, bathing, creating power, recreation, sacred cermonies, and waste disposal. All of these uses around the world are in some way related because of the connectedness of water, a vast but finite resource.

Challenge students to name three things that don't need water. Then ask, "Who or what *does* need water?" Some of their possible responses might include plants, animals, human, factories, and so on. "How do we use water in our homes and schools?" to which they might response: for cooking, washing, watering plants, flushing toilets, drinking, and so forth.

The average American family uses a surprising amount of water each day. Have the students and their parents use the data below to calculate the amount of water their households use. Discuss how many times a day each family performs an activity listed below, such as flushing the toilet, and multiply that number by the gallons used each time to get daily total for each activity.

	GALLONS
Toilet flushing	5
A short shower (five minutes)	25
Tub bath	35
Brushing teeth	2
Washing dishes with water running	30
Washing dishes in a basin	10
Using the dishwasher	20
One load of laundry	40

Brainstorm other ways families could figure out how much water their household uses in a day. Suggestions might include reading the water meter or measuring the amount of water collected in basins every time they turn on a faucet. Scholastic Voyages of Discovery's *Water: The Source of Life* offers quirky historical facts about bathing, plumbing, and clothes washing, as well as a whole minicourse of water information.

Children can set the example for water conservation. Suggest that they investigate how water is wasted in their households. They might look for leaky faucets, partial loads of dishes or laundry being washed, letting water run when washing dishes or teeth, and so on. Discuss ways we could conserve water around the house. Students could create a short slogan—small enough to xerox onto mailing labels—to remind others not to waste water. Then have them apply stickers wherever they see water being wasted.

Although only a small percentage of our daily water consumption is for drinking, it is an essential use. One glass of water equals eight ounces (one cup). Ask students, "How many glasses of water would you have to drink each day to equal one gallon? How much of our water consumption is for drinking?" Ask children if they have ever thought about what it would be like to run out of water. Most people can only survive for five to seven days with no water. Perhaps they could write a story about a season without water.

There are nearly six billion people on earth; at least three billion go without clean water. In some desert communities in Africa, whole families subsist on a few gallons of water a day. There it is the children's job to carry water from a central town well, often a long walk from home. One gallon of water weighs about 8.3 pounds. If each student in the class had to carry enough water to meet her family's daily needs, how much would it weigh?

In some places the water supply comes from a well or nearby reservoir; in other places it is piped in from hundreds of miles away. Interview parents, fellow students, teachers, and town officials. Do they know where their drinking water comes from (both for home and for school)?

There may be several different sources in one community. Survey the class or whole school to find out the source of their drinking supply. Graph the number of students and teachers who get their drinking water from wells, town supply, bottled water, or other sources.

Animals need water, too, as *Who Comes to the Water Hole?* by Colleen Stanley Bare illustrates with color photos of visitors to an African watering hole. During the dry season in southern Africa, many animals have to share a small watering hole fed by a spring. A mother and baby rhinoceros, warthogs, baboons, zebras, and birds are always alert for predators like lions, cheetahs, and hyenas that hunt near the watering hole.

Discuss how plants such as cacti and animals such as camels conserve water. Instead of sweating, a camel's body temperature rises as much as eleven degrees Fahrenheit (six degrees Celsius) on a hot day, and cools at night! What would happen to us if our body temperature changed so much so rapidly? Why are cacti called "green canteens"?

Water use, abuse, and conservation are different illustrations of the same concept: that all the water there is is all the water there is. How we have used water in the past and how we use it today will have an impact on those who have to use it again and again in succeeding generations.

How Humans Have Changed the Waterways

Jane Yolen researched how, in the early 1900s, several towns in western Massachusetts were drowned to supply water for metropolitan Boston. She recounts in *Letting Swift River Go* how seven towns were relocated, including their buildings and graves. Trees were cut down and dams constructed to flood a valley to create the Quabbin Reservoir. It is a poignant story that can lead to a discussion about how much we are willing to sacrifice for an adequate, convenient drinking water supply. Discuss how some parts of the country, especially those that have large populations or low rainfall, have a hard time getting enough water for their residents. By looking at a map of the United States, learners can predict where these places may be. They can also use an atlas to find out which areas have low annual rainfall. Class members can write to the Chambers of Commerce to find out how these communities manage to maintain an adequate water supply.

People have shaped the rivers by how they have used the water, its resources, and its shoreline. Lynne Cherry wrote *A River Ran Wild: An Environmental History* to document the effect, both good and bad, that human actions had on the Nashua River in Massachusetts. Small illustrations bordering each page provide clues for how the river was used by humans and what wildlife depended on it. The story begins in

1600 and continues through the present time. To make the story more meaningful, ask students to create a timeline using a long roll of paper, marking off the centuries. Invite them first to put on any other dates or events that are significant to them, such as when basketball was invented, their birth date, the year they will graduate, and so forth. Then challenge them to illustrate the changes, inventions, and river uses described or illustrated in the story. They may also want to refer to the timeline inside the cover of *A River Ran Wild*.

Discuss what people did to hurt and to help the Nashua River. Taking cues from actions that people took to restore that river, ask children what they could do to protect our rivers, lakes, and streams. Some possible answers include: conserve water, don't pollute, write letters to the editor, lobby legislators, make posters, teach others about the river, participate in shoreline cleanup events, and so on.

A River Ran Wild provides a good overview of the various cultures and industries that depended on waterways as do *Minn of the Mississippi* and *Paddle-to-the-Sea*. The exploration and discovery of America can be traced along its waterways. Its wild streams and curving rivers were the primary transportation routes inland from the sea for thousands of years. Not until the coming of the railroad did significant traffic patterns begin to radiate out beyond the river valleys.

Native Americans, of course, were the first to use these highways. Archeological excavations along streams and estuaries have unearthed arrowheads and kitchen middens—Native American garbage dumps—that mark their prehistoric campsites. The indigenous people identified portage sites where they had to carry their birchbark canoes over rapids and waterfalls, giving them names we still use today. *Abol,* an Abenaki word for rapids, translates to "where the water laughs in coming down." *Debsconeag,* a stretch of rapids on the West Branch of the Penobscot River, means "carrying place."

Like the American Indians, the first white explorers penetrated the wilderness by canoe. In the early 1600s, French explorer Samuel de Champlain followed the St. Lawrence River to discover the Great Lakes. The French adopted the Indian name for the St. Lawrence River, *Canada,* as the name for their new country. Champlain hoped to find a western water outlet from the Great Lakes, the Northwest Passage, to reach the Pacific Ocean. It wasn't until 1793, when English explorer Alexander Mackenzie completed an expedition through what is now British Columbia, that people gave up the dream of a freshwater highway linking both the Pacific and the Atlantic oceans.

In 1804, two U. S. Army officers, Lewis and Clark, set out to map the Northwestern frontier, from St. Louis, Missouri, to the Pacific Ocean. They journeyed up the Missouri River, across the Rocky Mountains, and along the Columbia and other rivers to the coast. They traveled a total of 8,000 miles, guided much of the way by Sacagawea, a Shoshone Indian woman.

The settlers who retraced the early explorers' water routes built dams to harness water power and launched log drives to transport timber to shipyards and sawmills. Logs, fur, fish, iron ore, and even ice floated down the nation's waterways to a growing coastal population. Gradually, this use took its toll. Eroding soil, sawdust, and timbers clogged the streams and filled in their depths. The rivers became dumping sites for the refuse of waterfront communities. Pipes pumped raw sewage and industrial pollutants directly into the water.

After centuries of abuse, the rivers reeked of offensive wastes. Communities began to invest their resources in cleaning up their waterways. Sewage treatment plants were installed or upgraded. Dams were breached or fitted with fish ladders so salmon could return to their ancestral spawning grounds upstream. New businesses based on clean water—including whitewater rafting, kayaking, and sport fishing—are pumping a stream of tourist dollars into communities bordering interior waterways.

Using a map or satellite image of the United States and Canada, see how much of the way across the continent you can trace over water routes. Discuss how the history of the exploration of our continent would have been different if Champlain and Lewis and Clark had had satellite images and navigational aids to guide them. Discuss how the rivers and lands they charted have changed since 1804.

A pollution mystery

As a follow-up to reading *A River Ran Wild*, you can create your own pollution story. By adding their own pollutants to a container of clean water in the classroom, students can graphically illustrate the sources of pollution in rivers, lakes, and other bodies of water. Although some pollution is from factories and town sewage treatment plants, much of it is caused by ordinary people.

Create a story that includes many different "polluters," like the sample scenario below. Start with a large clear bowl or aquarium of clean water, a long-handled spoon, and either film canisters or baby food jars containing various forms of "pollution" described in parentheses. You may need to make duplicates to ensure that each child has a role. (I like to use film canisters because the students can't see what's inside before opening them up.) All "pollutants" should be able to be flushed down the toilet without straining one's local sewage system: Avoid things like paint or motor oil.

Distribute small vials or jars of materials to class members. Explain that each vial is marked with the name of a character in the story. Use the name of a local pond, river, or reservoir that may be familiar to your students. As a student's character is mentioned, he or she should go to front of room and add the contents of vial to a large container of water as the teacher (or a student) reads the story. After each packet is emptied into the water, stir the mixture with a long-handled spoon.

This is the story of a swift river that was named "Running Free" by the Native Americans. They lived along its shores and hunted and fished. Sometimes the remains of their feasts washed into the water. [Add shell fragments.] But it wasn't much.

The Native Americans built their camps next to the river because they knew that even in a heavy rainstorm, the wetland grasses that grew along the shore would soak up the runoff like a sponge and keep their camp from flooding. They cleared small plots of land for gardens.

Then European settlers came. They cut down the trees along the shoreline to open up land for farming. Soil washed into the river because there were no longer trees to hold it back. [Add soil.]

Farmers grew crops along the shoreline and used fertilizers to help grow corn, potatoes, strawberries, and so forth. [Add baking soda.]

Along the banks of a fast-flowing stream that flowed into the river a miller built a dam to harness water power to turn the water wheel in his mill. He and his workers used the energy of the water to power machinery to grind corn. Some of the flour got into the water. [Add flour.]

Nearby, a shoemaker used chemicals to make the leather soft and flexible so he could make sturdy shoes. Some of the chemicals washed into the river. [Add food coloring and vinegar.]

A lumberjack used the water to carry logs to a sawmill to make wood to build homes and bridges. Some of the bark, wood, and sawdust sank to the bottom and decayed. [Add sawdust and wood chips.]

Bacteria that attacked the wood and sawdust used up a lot of the oxygen in the water that the fish needed. [Add gummy fish or fish-shaped crackers.]

Soon other residents built houses along the shore. Where did they dump their sewage? Into the water. [Add raisins and small bits of toilet paper.] At first, the bacteria in the mud could clean up the sewage. But before long, too much sewage overloaded the river's ability to break it down into nutrients that the plants could use to grow.

One of these homeowners was a gardener who was very proud of her unusual plants and large lawn stretching to the water's edge. She used fertilizers and insecticides to keep them green and healthy. [Add cocoa.]

Next door whenever a driver washed his car, he didn't notice that all the phosphate soap ran down his driveway into the water. [Add dishwashing liquid.]

Some <u>school students</u> out on a field trip were doing a scavenger hunt along the river. A gust of wind tore their worksheets from their hands and carried them out over the water. [Add bits of paper.]

At a nearby service station, a <u>gas station attendant</u> spilled some oil as he was changing the oil filter on a car. Some of it washed downhill into the water. [Add coffee mixed with cooking oil.]

One day, a <u>sailor</u> went out onto the river and discovered it wasn't clean and clear anymore. [Place tiny plastic or clay sailboat on top.]

"Who polluted this water?" she cried.

What was the answer? "We all did."

And we all can do something about it.

Challenge students to write a version of the story suggesting ways to prevent or clean up the pollution.

Cleaning up pollution

How do we clean up pollution? In the *The Magic School Bus at the Waterworks*, Ms. Frizzle's students follow water through a sewage treatment plant: through a mixing basin, settling basin, and sand and gravel filters to a storage tank, then through a water main and out through a faucet in the girls' bathroom at school. Another choice, *Flush!! Treating Wastewater* by K. M. Coombs, is a photographic journey that traces wastewater after it is flushed down the toilet.

Help children understand that they can be part of the solution. To demonstrate, create a "living" sewage treatment plant using students, mime, photos, and props to illustrate how a drop of water gets cleaned up. A sample script might go like this:

"Where does water go when you flush the toilet?" (Hold up a toilet seat cover.) A *water drop* (student dressed in a blue shirt with small baggies of "sewage"—dirt or brown construction paper—taped to shirt and holding a stick) travels through *pipes* underground (plastic pipe) that carry the water to the sewage treatment plant (a large box with words SEWAGE TREATMENT FACILITY).

First, sewage passes through a *screen* (window screen) that removes large objects. ("Water drop" student drops stick.) Then put into the water in the mixing basin, a chemical called *alum* (someone mimes pouring from a bottle marked ALUM and another student stirs with a wooden spoon) that will stick to the sewage to make it sink to the bottom of the basin. (Drops another bag.) Here tiny bacteria are waiting to eat the sludge that sinks to the bottom. (Kneeling students simulate munching action.) The water continues on through *sand* and *gravel* filters. (Shake containers of sand and gravel.) Then chlorine and fluoride are added to the water. (Students pretend to pour from other bottles as the "Water drop" drops the last bag of "sewage.") What do theses chemicals do? (Kill any remaining disease germs and help prevent cavities.) Eventually, the cleaned-up water flows through another *pipe* to the school where a student drinks part of it and then starts the process all over again (student drinks a glass of water) by pouring the water down the drain. (Repeat the process.) Eventually, the water flows into the ocean (show picture) where fish and other creatures swim in it. (Use illustrations or props of sea creatures or simulate swimming or crab claws.)

Students can make their own water filters by punching small holes in the bottom of paper cups using opened paper clips. Layer from the bottom up: pebbles, coarse sand, charcoal, cotton balls. Add some dirt to a glass of water and stir until cloudy. Pour it through the filter over a collecting basin to catch the water. Ask, "Is it clean?" Compare the filtered water with the muddy water. What happens when students filter the water again?

What can filters alone clean? (Particles that can be strained out.) What can't they remove? (Dissolved pollutants and microorganisms.) What parts of the sewage treatment process takes care of dissolved pollutants? (Chlorine and other chemicals are added before the water is released into the ocean or river.)

Invite an employee of the local sewage treatment plant to visit (or visit her!) to learn where your drinking water comes from, where it goes, how it is cleaned at both ends of the distribution cycle. Ask your visitor how the local sewage treatment plant is similar and different from the facility Ms. Frizzle toured with her students or that the photographer followed in *Flush!!*

As children begin to understand how much effort it takes to clean up water, they can easily appreciate how much better it would be if we kept our rivers cleaner in the first place.

Kids as caretakers

Children can contribute in significant ways to keeping waterways clean. In Frank Asch's *Up River*, for example, student volunteers spend a day canoeing on Otter Creek observing wildlife and cleaning up garbage with retired teacher Mike. They see a mallard, an osprey, a weasel, a frog, a raccoon, and a beaver. Their efforts, they hope, will help make Otter Creek hospitable for otters again. This book helps launch a class discussion about how we can keep our rivers, lakes, and oceans clean.

Many students, especially at the high school level, are involved in water quality monitoring. A high school science teacher or student, a local lake or other conservation organization, or the state agency responsible for environmental protection may provide information about water quality monitoring in your area. Many of the tests—such as water temperature, pH (acidity or alkalinity), dissolved oxygen, salinity, and turbidity (water clarity)—can be done by elementary students. Water-testing kits, available through science supply catalogs, have simple chemical tests elementary students can use effectively.

In some communities, students map valuable wetlands by looking at aerial photos or satellite images of their town and "ground truthing" the images by going out into the field to find and map these water bodies.

Students often organize beach cleanup days to pick up garbage from along the shoreline of beaches and rivers. All participants should wear gloves and be alerted that leaking barrels and other suspicious refuse should be left alone. You might brainstorm a list of the kinds of pollution they may expect to find and make that into a check-off sheet. A scribe in each group can keep a tally of the items found (i.e., plastic, soda and beer cans, cigarette butts, fishing gear, and so on). When they return to class, they can use the data to create graphs or fraction and percentage problems.

Children's concern for water habitats quickly spills over into environmental issues confronting the ocean, which has some of these problems: pollution, overharvesting, and overcrowding of the shoreline.

But it is not just its water issues or water concepts that are important to convey to learners, it is the allure and mystery of water in all its guises. As science writer Loren Eiseley wrote in *The Immense Journey*, "If there is magic on this planet, it is contained in water. . . . Its substance reaches everywhere; it touches the past and prepares the future; it moves under the poles and wanders thinly in the heights of air. It can assume forms of exquisite perfection in a snowflake, or strip the living to a single shining bone cast upon the sea" (1957, 16–17).

Children's Books Cited

ASCH, FRANK. 1995. *Up River*. New York: Simon & Schuster Books for Young Readers.

BARE, COLLEEN STANLEY. 1991. *Who Comes to the Water Hole?* New York: Cobblehill Books.

BLACKISTONE, MICK. 1991. *The Day They Left the Bay*. Tracys Landing, MD: Blue Crab Press.

BUCK, L. 1974. *Wetlands: Bogs, Marshes, and Swamps*. New York: Parents' Magazine Press.

BURNS, DIANE. 1994. *Cranberries: Fruit of the Bogs*. Minneapolis, MN: Carolrhoda Books.

CAITLIN, STEPHEN. 1990. *Wonders of Swamps and Marshes*. Mahwah, NJ: Troll Associates.

CHASE, EDITH. 1995. *Waters*. Buffalo: NY: Firefly Books.

CHERRY, LYNNE. 1992. *A River Ran Wild: An Environmental History*. San Diego: Harcourt Brace Juvenile Books.

COBB, VICKI. 1986. *The Trip of a Drip*. Boston: Little, Brown.

COLE, JOANNA. 1986. *The Magic School Bus at the Waterworks*. New York: Scholastic.

CONE, MOLLY. 1992. *Come Back, Salmon*. San Francisco: Sierra Club Books.

COOMBS, K. M. 1995. *Flush!! Treating Wastewater*. Minneapolis, MN: Carolrhoda Books.

CUMMINGS, PRISCILLA. 1986. *Chadwick the Crab*. Centreville, MD: Tidewater Publications.

———. 1991. *Sid and Sal's Famous Channel Marker Diner*. Centreville, MD: Tidewater Publishers.

CUTCHINS, JUDY, and GINNY JOHNSTON. 1989. *Scoots, The Bog Turtle*. New York: Atheneum Books for Young Readers.

DAY, NANCY. 1992. *The Horseshoe Crab*. New York: Dillon Press.

DEWEY, JENNIFER OWINGS. 1987. *At the Edge of the Pond*. Boston: Little, Brown.

DORROS, ARTHUR. 1991. *Follow the Water from Brook to Ocean*. New York: HarperCollins Children's Books.

GANS, ROMA. 1973. *Water for Dinosaurs and You*. New York: Crowell Junior Books.

GEORGE, WILLIAM, and LINDSAY GEORGE. 1988. *Beaver at Long Pond*. New York: Greenwillow Books.

GEORGE, WILLIAM. 1989. *Box Turtle at Long Pond*. New York: Greenwillow Books.

GLOB, P. V. 1965. *The Bog People*. Ithaca, NY: Cornell University Press.

GOLDIN, AUGUSTA. 1989. *Ducks Don't Get Wet*. New York: Harper Trophy.

HIRSCHI, RON. 1991. *Loon Lake*. New York: Cobblehill Books.

HOLLING, HOLLING C. 1980. *Paddle-to-the-Sea*. Boston: Houghton Mifflin.

———. 1992. *Minn of the Mississippi*. Boston: Houghton Mifflin.

LANE, MARGARET. 1982. *The Fish: Story of the Stickleback*. New York: Dial Press.

LAVIES, BIANCA. 1989. *Lily Pad Pond*. New York: Dutton Children's Books.

———. 1992. *The Atlantic Salmon*. New York: Dutton Children's Books.

LOCKER, THOMAS. 1993. *Where the River Begins*. New York: Puffin Books.

MacDonald, Amy. 1990. *Little Beaver and the Echo*. New York: G. P. Putnam's Sons.

McCloskey, Robert. 1976. *Make Way for Ducklings*. New York: Puffin Books.

Milne, Lorus, and Margery Milne. 1984. *Mystery of the Bog Forest*. New York: Dodd Mead and Company.

Parker, Steve. 1988. *Pond and River*. New York: Knopf Books for Young Readers.

Pringle, Laurence. 1973. *Estuaries: Where Rivers Meet the Sea*. New York: MacMillan.

Rauzon, Mark, and Cynthia Overbeck Bix. 1994. *Water, Water Everywhere*. San Francisco: Sierra Club Books.

Robbins, Ken. 1994. *Water*. New York: Henry Holt & Company.

Robertson, Kayo. 1986. *Signs Along the River: Learning to Read the Natural Landscape*. Boulder, Colorado: Roberts Rinehart Publishing Group.

Rosenfeld, Sam. 1970. *A Drop of Water*. Irvington on Hudson, NY: Harvey House.

Schmid, Eleanore. 1990. *The Water's Journey*. New York: North-South Books.

Scholastic, Voyages of Discovery series. 1995. *Water: The Source of Life*. New York: Scholastic.

Seuss, Dr. [Theodor Geisel]. 1947. *McElligot's Pool*. New York: Random House Books for Young Readers.

Stidworthy, John. 1990. *Ponds and Streams*. Mahwah, NJ: Troll Associates.

Tate, Suzanne. 1991. *Harry Horseshoe Crab: A Tale of Crawly Creatures*. Nags Head, NC: Nags Head Art.

Waters, John. 1970. *The Crab from Yesterday*. New York: Frederick Warne & Company.

Weinberger, Jane. 1992. *Cory the Cormorant*. Mount Desert, ME: Windswept House Publications.

Wexler, Jerome. 1994. *Sundew Stranglers: Plants That Eat Insects*. New York: Dutton Children's Books.

Wilcox, Charlotte. 1993. *Mummies and Their Mysteries*. Minneapolis, MN: Carolrhoda Books.

Yolen, Jane. 1992. *Letting Swift River Go*. Boston: Little, Brown.

Zion, Gene. 1988. *Dear Garbage Man*. New York: Trumpet Book Club.

5 Ocean

Where do you begin a study of the ocean? The ocean is such a fascinating, all-encompassing topic that you could teach all subjects all year long using the theme of the sea. And there are plenty of trade books to help with the task. For example, *Sea Squares* and *Sea Sums,* both by Joy Hulme, use ocean creatures to teach about mathematics. *Is a Blue Whale the Biggest Thing There Is?* by Robert Wells addresses both science and math, using the hundred-foot-long blue whale as a scale by which to measure Mt. Everest. Trade books about the ocean can take you across all disciplines, across all seas, and from the shoreline to the deep ocean vents. Because textbooks about the ocean have to cover so much material, they by necessity give short shrift to individual topics. By using children's literature to explore the ocean, you can can focus on the areas you want to study "in depth."

One way to start a unit on the the marine world is to ask students to make a list of ways that the ocean is different from the land. Answers like "wet," "cold," "dark," "can't breathe there" may reveal our human limitations in surviving underwater, yet many animals find it the easiest place on earth to live, because

The ocean is three-dimensional. It can support life at any level. On earth, unless you are a bird, your living space is pretty much restricted to the surface of the earth. Not only does an animal have more personal space in the sea, so does its food supply.

The ocean provides buoyancy. The density of water supports the vast weight of ships and whales.

The ocean is stable. Water temperature and other physical factors change slowly, if at all, providing a stable environment for living creatures. Because the ocean has changed little over many millennia, marine animals have had a long time to adapt to some of the challenges of ocean living, like the extreme pressure and darkness of the deep sea.

Water circulates food, nutrients, animals—and pollution. Only land barriers like islands and continents thwart the continuous movement of water around the globe. If you drew a line around a globe, you could trace across all the oceans with one continuous line. All the oceans, like all the world's water, are connected. You might help students appreciate this fact better by giving them another map of the world, which doesn't label the oceans. Ask them to locate the Atlantic Ocean, Pacific Ocean, Indian Ocean, Arctic Ocean, and Southern (Antarctic) Ocean.

Life flourishes in many parts of the sea, particularly where there is light and food. Although most life is concentrated in the shallow parts of the sea, living creatures can even be found in the deep ocean vents, where minerals from volcanic vents nurture unusual life forms. You should explain to students that nutrients and food in the sea include minerals, chemicals, and decaying matter, as well as the forms of nourishment that they typically think of as food.

Exploring the Ocean

The Magic School Bus on the Ocean Floor is a fine jumping-off point, literally, for exploring the ocean as Ms. Frizzle steers the Magic School Bus under the waves. Joanna Cole's text and Bruce Degen's illustrations provide an overview of ocean habitats, some of the physical parameters, ocean food chains, and several notable creatures of the sea. Back in class, Ms. Frizzle's students create a bulletin board of the ocean floor.

Your study of the oceans could itself be an ocean journey, starting with the coastal habitats of estuaries, beaches, and tidepools, then moving out to coral reefs, temperate and cold seas, the frigid Arctic and Antarctic oceans, down to the deepest reaches of the sea, where oceanographers have found a whole new world not based on photosynthesis. Along the way you can have students investigate individual ocean creatures and the adaptations that have made them successful in the sea. A vast array of books can help introduce students to the marine world. Robert Kraske's *The Voyager's Stone: The Adventures of a Message Carrying Bottle Adrift on the Ocean Sea* tells of a boy, vacationing in the Caribbean, who puts a message and a pebble into a bottle and throws the bottle into the sea. It drifts along the East Coast of the United States on the Gulf Stream and up north to the Arctic, east across the Atlantic and down through the Sargasso Sea, south to Antarctica and into the Indian Ocean until it is retrieved by a little girl in Australia. This book gives students a reason to find the oceans of the world on a globe and to learn about how currents circulate around the globe.

Getting Started

In this chapter, after an overview of the ocean, we'll explore five ocean ecosystems (beaches, tidepools, temperate and cold seas, coral reefs, and the Antarctic Ocean) and then target specific marine animals representing different animal groups that appeal to children:

penguins (birds)

lobsters (invertebrates)

fishes (bony fishes)

sharks (cartilaginous fishes)

whales (marine mammals)

Finally we'll wrap up by looking at people and the seas and the effects of pollution.

To get started, you can help learners appreciate the vast amount of water on earth by making a wall map of the world using green rug scraps to show the land and blue rug scraps or other nubby material to show the sea. You can then have students stand a few feet away and toss a Velcro-covered ball at the map. Have them record the number of times the ball hits blue and and the number of times it hits green. What percentage of the throws hit the blue oceans? Is the proportion roughly equal to three quarters, the approximate area of the earth's surface covered by ocean?

An alphabet book, *Under the Sea from A to Z*, written by Anne Doubilet, shows photos by her husband, National Geographic photographer David Doubilet. *The Ocean Alphabet Book* and *The Underwater Alphabet Book*, both by Jerry Pallotta, feature a host of marine animals, with text that often mentions where they are found. These books can help your students begin making a collection of animals to include in an ocean mural like the one in Ms. Frizzle's class. *Land Under the Sea* by Hershell Nixon and Joan Lowery Nixon will help them make sure the mural accurately depicts the depths—*bathymetry*—of the ocean floor. It explains how oceanographers identified undersea features like the continental shelf, the continental slope, ocean trenches, ocean basins, plateaus, and mid-ocean ridges.

Before World War II, very little was known about the oceans. It was assumed that the ocean floor was flat; today we know its valleys and mountains can be more dramatic than any on land. Until the invention of sonar, oceanographers mapped the depths of the ocean by dropping a weighted plumb line over the side of a ship and measuring the length of rope that was let out. These measurements of the ocean's depth were called *soundings*. This technique is comparable to someone trying to map the continental United States by lowering a rope every fifty miles or so from an airplane as it flies over the country.

To make this clearer, you can have students do their own soundings to create a profile of the seafloor. Line a row of cardboard boxes against one wall of the classroom. Pile several boxes on top of each other to create different heights. Suspend a blue shower curtain or row of butcher block paper in front of the boxes to a height above the eye level of the children (so they can't see what's behind). Mark off one-foot intervals on five-foot-long dowels for students to use as "sounding rods."

Then have students examine a chart of the seafloor (and the *Magic School Bus on the Ocean Floor*) and pick out geologic features like the continental shelf, the continental slope, a sea mount, a trench, an oceanic ridge, a plain, and so on. Have the students start at one end of the curtain. At two-foot intervals, have them take a measurement of the "depth" by poking a thin dowel straight down behind the curtain. Have the children call out the depth of each sample to a partner who records the number. Back at their seats have the pair create a bathymetric chart by placing their measurements on graph paper and connecting the points. Explain that each mark on the dowel is equal to, say, ten thousand feet in depth and each two-foot interval on the floor is equal to 500 miles of horizontal distance.

The Tides

Although most of the rest of the ocean is stable, the shoreline definitely is not. The edge of the sea is constantly under assault by wind, weather, waves, and tides.

Why do the tides change? One answer is provided in *Why the Tides Ebb and Flow* by Joan Chase Bowden. An Old Woman removes a rock from the hole in the sea and the sea begins to pour down and down into the bottomless pit that was the hole in the sea. The Sky Spirit sends a Little Dog, a Young Maiden, and a Young Man to close the hole in the sea, but the Old Woman adopts them as her family. Put back the rock, promises the Sky Spirit, and I will let you borrow the rock twice each day to pretty up your garden. The Old Woman agrees. When the rock is removed, it creates low tide. When the Old Woman puts the rock back in place, the sea fills up to create high tide.

Like most legends, this one has some basis in fact. Along most coastlines, the tides rise and fall twice each day. Locate a tide chart from a boating supply store. Look at low tide for the day you want to go to the beach. Is it in the morning or the afternoon? How early or late? Some tide charts list different times for the high and low tide for different locations along the coast. Why are the tides different at different places? (The shape of the coastline influences the height and arrival time of high tides. In the funnel-like Bay of Fundy, for instance, the difference between high tide and low tide is over forty feet, but a few hundred miles south, on Nantucket Island, the tidal range is only a foot.) Ask students, "If you want to have lots of room on the beach to frolic or to beachcomb, when would be the best time for you to go? If you want to launch a boat into the water, when should you arrive?"

The tides are caused by the gravitational tug-of-war between the moon and the earth. The moon's gravity pulls on the water—and to a lesser degree, on the land as well—on the side of the earth that is facing it. Thus, high tide occurs when the moon is directly overhead. On the opposite side of the world, the spinning of the earth causes the water to move away from the earth, creating another high tide on the other side of the world. Halfway between these two high tides are areas where the water is low—the low tides.

The sun also pulls on the earth, but because it is so far away, its tug is only about half as strong as the moon's. When the sun and moon are in line with each other (around the time of the new moon and the full moon), their gravitational effects combine to cause especially high and low tides, called *spring tides*. Spring tides get their name from an Anglo-Saxon word *sprungen,* to "spring forward." Spring tides have nothing to do with the seasons. They occur twice every month. At the quarter and three quarter moons, the earth and sun are at right angles to each other, cancelling out some of their effect. The tides at these times are neither especially high or low; the difference between high and low tide is the smallest. These are known as *neap tides.* Using different sizes of Christmas ornaments for the sun, moon, and earth, have students construct a mobile of spring and neap tides.

To show how tides on the earth bulge when they are directly under the moon, place one student in the center of the room to be the earth. Have him hold an eight-foot length of rope with the ends tied together at waist level to represent the water that envelops the earth. Have another student (the "moon") walk around the earth slowly, pulling the rope around as he moves. Another student standing opposite the moon also walks around the earth at the same pace, pulling on the rope, representing the bulge opposite the side of the earth on which the moon pulls, the result of centrifugal force. Explain that the oceans, because they cover three quarters of the earth's surface, are like an envelope of water around the globe. The gravitational force of the moon pulls the envelope toward it and centrifugal force pulls it away.

Along with the tides, waves rule the shoreline and the creatures that attempt to live there. To make waves in a bottle, fill a clear bottle two thirds full with water tinted blue with food coloring. Then fill the jar to the top with clear vegetable or mineral oil. Screw on the cap tightly and rock the bottle back and forth to create slow-motion waves. (Note that the bottle is too small to create a breaking wave.)

Tidepools

The tidepool is our window into the sea where we can sit quietly and watch marine creatures struggle for shelter, food, and protection. It is a miniature ocean ruled by the tides. At first glance, a tidepool seems only to be filled with seaweeds, barnacles, and mussels. But a closer look may reveal sea stars and sea urchins hiding under curtains of seaweed, while crabs scuttle from beneath rocks to attack anything that moves and stinging sea anemones extend their tentacles into the water, waiting for the waves to deliver their next meal.

Pounding waves at high tide and drying sun at low tide make the tidepool one of the hardest places in the ocean to survive. Yet animals and plants have found ways to beat the waves, heat, and hungry predators. Starfish, limpets, and sea urchins cling to rocks with suction-cup feet, while barnacles use their own brand of Super Glue. Mussels throw lassos to tie themselves to the rocks. In fact, every inch of the tidepool is covered with life because the tidepool offers what most of the open ocean can not: plenty of light for plant growth (because it's shallow) and nutrients—decaying matter and minerals washed in from the land.

Any unit on tidepools should include:

- Zonation: The area where each plant and animal lives in the tidepool depends on how long it can stay out of water.

- Adaptations: The ingenious ways that tidepool animals and plants have evolved to hold on, keep from drying out, and protect themselves from enemies.

- Food chains: The ways grazing vegetarians, carnivorous hunters, and animals that can't move at all get their food.

Mary Adrian's *A Day and a Night in a Tidepool,* Sheila Cole's *When the Tide Is Low,* Anita Malnig's *Where the Waves Break: Life at the Edge of the Sea,* and Jeanne Bendick's *Exploring an Ocean Tide Pool* are all fine introductions to these aspects of tidepools. The best description of individual species is found in *The Seaside Naturalist* by Deborah A. Coulombe, where each creature gets its own page of facts interspersed with occasional quizzes. Mimi Gregoire Carpenter provides a beautifully illustrated guide for beachcombers of what washes up onshore in *What the Sea Left Behind*. Her finely detailed watercolors of broken shells and seaweed show them as the treasures they are. Mimi Carpenter takes a more fanciful approach to tidepools in *Mermaid in a Tidal Pool*, the story of a lonely little girl who finds her soulmate in a tidepool.

Using trade books, have learners select various animals or plants that are found in a tidepool to study. Ask them to figure out how each holds on against the waves at high tide, keeps from drying out when the tide is low, and protects itself from predators. Ask them to figure out where in the tidepool each organism can be found. The class can then make a mural of the tidepool placing an illustration of the animal or algae at the zone where it can be found.

Food chains get their due in *What's for Lunch? The Eating Habits of Seashore Creatures* by Sam and Beryl Epstein. *Seashores* by Joyce Pope also describes what some seashore animals of the tidepool and beach eat. Have children research at least one thing that their tidepool creature eats and an animal that eats them. You should make sure that at least some children cover plankton—an important part of the ocean food chain—and algae, called seaweeds—plants that get their energy from the sun and that a number of tidepool creatures feed on. Have each child make up a picture of her animal or plant. Starting with the sun, construct a food web by connecting string between all the animals and plants that eat or provide food for one another. (This is easier to do if you have all the students sitting in a circle.) You might insert a human into the food web, as we eat many things that live in the tidepool, including seaweed!

Have you had your seaweed today?

Traditionally, Irish moss pudding, or *blanc mange*, has been a tasty treat from the sea. Irish moss (*Chondrus crispus*) is a red algae that grows in the low tide zone. Its stubby, branching fronds reflect an iridescent sheen when you see them slightly below the water's surface. Years ago, Irish moss was harvested with long-handled rakes and sold to manufacturers to be incorporated into many food products. Even if you have never eaten Irish moss pudding, you've probably eaten seaweed. *Carrageenan* is used as a thickener in puddings and as a stabilizer to keep suspensions from separating. It is found in chocolate milk, ice cream, whipped cream, milk shakes, puddings, and toothpaste! Have students scour the supermarket looking for carrageenan, particularly among the ingredients in their favorite desserts.

Making seaweed pudding not only satisfies the culinary adventurers in your class, it fills your room with the tangy aroma of the sea. Pick Irish moss only from tidepools where you know the water is clean and where collecting is allowed. You can also use the bleached Irish moss that washes up on shore, or buy powdered Irish moss or carrageenan from health food stores.

> 1 quart milk
> generous handful of Irish moss (about one cup)
> $1/2$ cup sugar*
> 1 teaspoon vanilla*
> $1/2$ teaspoon salt
>
> *You may substitute $1/2$ cup maple syrup for sugar and vanilla.

Soak clean Irish moss in cold water for 15 minutes and then put it into a cheesecloth bag. Add the bag to four cups of milk in a double boiler. Cook over boiling water for 15-20 minutes, stirring constantly. Add sugar and salt and stir for another 5-10 minutes. Remove the pan from the stove and discard Irish moss. Add vanilla. Cool and eat.

Tidepool animals

One tidepool animal that is the subject of many children's books is the hermit crab. You might be inspired to keep a land hermit crab in a classroom aquarium after reading any of these charming stories about their marine cousins: Holling Clancey Holling's story-cum-marine-biology-text, *Pagoo*, Michael Glaser's *Does Anyone Know Where a Hermit Crab Goes?*, Eric Carle's *A House for Hermit Crab*, and Megan McDonald's *Is This a House for Hermit Crab?* All of these explain that a hermit crab must leave its borrowed shell and find a new one as the hermit grows. Unlike its relatives, the crabs and lobsters, the hermit crab must use someone else's shell to protect its soft rear end. The claws and front of its body are covered by its own exoskeleton, which is shed and regrows as it increases in size.

Tidepool trip

If possible, take your students to a tidepool for a culminating activity. When you plan a field trip to the tidepool, make sure to schedule it around a convenient low tide. You can make an underwater viewer to peek into tidepools from a coffee can with both ends cut off. Cover one end with plastic wrap and secure it in place with a large rubber band or duct tape. (Bring extra plastic wrap for field repairs.) Use duct tape to fasten a kitchen strainer to a long-handled broom to make a collecting net for deep tidal pools.

Beaches

Compared to estuaries and tidepools, sandy beaches sport little in the way of intertidal life, but they are the coastal habitat children are most familiar with from summers at the shore. *Sand in My Shoes* by Wendy Kesselman builds on this kinship. It is a little girl's good-bye to the seashore as she returns to the city at the end of the summer. *Beach Feet* by Lynn Reiser is a great introduction to exploring the beach. All the images of beach discoveries are seen as if you are looking down between your toes.

To learn how different animals use the beach, check out Mary Stoltz's *Night of Ghosts and Hermits: Nocturnal Life on the Seashore*. Photographer/author Bruce McMillan's *A Beach for the Birds* documents how least terns, an endangered species, nest on beaches that are set aside from people and their pollution.

One thing you can focus on at the beach is the sand. Ask children to recall how hot the sand can feel on their feet—the temperature of the sand can reach 120°F (48°C)! Ask them to imagine how hard it must be for beach creatures to survive in this hot place. Why do you think they burrow under the sand? Answers may reflect the need to find cooler temperatures, to escape the waves, and to hide from predators.

Newberry: The Life and Times of a Maine Clam by Vincent Dethier is sufficient reason alone to study the beach and adjoining mudflats. Newberry is a clam with a purple woolen muffler and an attitude. His ostentatious purple scarf gets him into and out of considerable trouble. He spends most of his time arguing or battling with his neighbors on the mudflat, including barnacles, sea gulls, starfishes, mussels, shrimp, and others. Written by a zoologist, *Newberry* is as accurate as it is entertaining. It's one of those after-lunch, read-aloud books that students beg you to read one more chapter.

Warm temperatures and drying winds can make a beach feel like a desert. As a matter of fact, many of the beach plants that grow in the sand dunes do resemble plants that you might find growing in the desert. Beach plants have evolved effective means to store water and keep moisture from evaporating from their leaves. Look in a field guide or go on a beach field trip to find an example among the dune plants of fuzzy leaves; thick, waxy leaves (like cactus); narrow, rolled-up leaves (beach grass, for example); and plants with pale leaves to reflect the sun's heat. Discuss how these adaptations help plants keep from losing moisture.

To learn about the landward margins of the beach, read Jan Gumbrecht Bannan's *Sand Dunes*. The author describes the formation and movement of dunes, as well as the different minerals that one can find in beach sand depending on where you live, such as feldspar, quartz, garnet, calcite, and gypsum. Sherry Garland's *The Summer Sands* highlights the importance of dunes as children launch a campaign to restore the fragile dunes by recycling Christmas trees to anchor blowing sand.

Ask students if they have ever examined beach sand with a hand lens. Collect a small quantity of beach sand and spread some on a piece of paper. Have them look for minerals and seashells. Where granite is a common rock, the minerals in sand are the component minerals of granite: quartz (clear, glassy, jagged), mica (shiny flakes), feldspar (a tan, pink, or white mineral), and hornblende (dark and dull-colored). In other places, the beach sand may be ground-up volcanic rock, coral, or seashells.

Over the course of the school year, have students make a collection of sand from different beaches by taping a pinch of sand to an index card. Label the card with the name of the beach, town, state, and date. The clear tape will allow them to view the sand through a hand lens or microscope. They could make up an extra sample to use as trading cards with friends or pen pals.

Compared to most ocean habitats, the sandy beach seems a barren place. If you want to find an abundance of life, look to the opposite ends of the ocean—cold-water seas and tropical coral reefs.

Tropical Seas vs. Temperate Seas

If you ask people to picture where in the ocean the largest number of fish are concentrated, most would think of the tropics, conjuring up images of a vivid, bustling coral reef. But consider the locations of the major fisheries of the world, which depend on netting large quantities of fish in each tow: cold waters. In the temperate and cold seas, relatively few species of animals but many individuals live, while in tropical waters, though the variety of life is astounding, there are far fewer individuals belonging to each species.

Though cold ocean waters offer a smaller variety of habitats (mainly ocean floor or open water) for a few species, there's more than enough food to nourish huge schools of tuna, cod, and mackerel. Nutrients from the land are carried by rivers to the sea where they fertilize the cold waters and promote the growth of tiny plants. These in turn feed tiny animals, which are eaten by small fishes that are eaten by larger fishes, on up the food chain. Cold water also holds more dissolved oxygen and carbon dioxide, gases that animals and plants respectively need, than warm water can. This rich soup of plankton—microscopic plants and animals—and decaying matter that are the base of the ocean food chain make cold northern waters appear murky.

The major fisheries of the world are located in cold seas because of the abundance of life here. Gail Gibbons's *Surrounded by Sea: Life on a New England Fishing Island* describes the importance of fishing in many northern coastal communities. Unfortunately, overfishing has changed not only the ecology but the economy of whole regions.

City Fish vs. Country Fish

I like to think of the contrast between fishes from cold seas and those from tropical seas as the "country fish" and the "city fish."

Cold-water fish

Cold-water fish are like "country fish": they live close to the earth, dress in drab colors, and follow the rhythms of the seasons. These fish tend to be full-bodied and streamlined, built for swimming long distances in large schools, or they may be adapted to living on the ocean floor. Common food fish, such as cod, haddock, and flounder, are called *groundfish* because they live close to the bottom. Cold-water fishes tend to be dull-colored (brown, black, or speckled) to match the sand or the seaweed, or silvery to reflect back the light under water. (Typically, schooling fish are silver.) Schools of cold-water fishes range across broad expanses of ocean, while the "city dwellers" of the coral reef compete for cramped quarters.

Coral reef fish

A coral reef is like a city in a desert—an oasis—which may provide the only food and shelter for many miles around. Tropical waters are crystal clear, with almost nothing suspended in the water to refract light or block our view. In other words, they're empty, except for the coral reef comunities.

Coral reef fish are like "city fish"— they live in tight quarters at well-defined levels; they are colorful, active night and day, and form complex and sometimes unusual associations and specializations. Reef fishes occupy many different levels, like apartment dwellers in high-rise buildings. Because they live crowded together, they have developed specializations in color or behavior (territoriality, symbiosis, nocturnal behavior, and so on) or design (venomous, bright colors) to help them defend their space on the reef. Coral reef fishes are often disc-shaped, flattened from side to side so they can slip into crevices in the reef. Coral reef fishes tend to be brightly colored to attract a mate, to advertise their services (such as a cleaner fish), to warn others away because they are territorial or venomous (such as a lionfish), or simply to blend in with the neon colors of the reef. Read the tale of "The City Mouse and the Country Mouse" and ask students to compare that story with the city fish and the country fish concept. Perhaps they could update the tale with a marine version.

Contrasting cold-water and coral reef fish

Challenge students to design a fish adapted for the coral reef and another for cold marine environments. Show them illustrations of tropical and cold marine fishes from a chart of cold marine fishes, a field guide to tropical marine fishes, an aquarium guide, or a handbook. Ask students where they think each fish would live—in cold seas like the northern Atlantic or Pacific or in warm tropical regions. Why? Explain that the purposes of fishes' coloration patterns, shapes, and adaptations are for protection, feeding, and finding a mate.

Discuss the task of a scientific illustrator who must accurately record and detail species of life. When a scientific illustrator draws a fish, he usually makes the illustration with the fish's head pointing to the left. (It's just accepted practice.) The artist's rendering may be the first view the world gets of a newly discovered species. You might mention that the field notes and illustrations of naturalists like Charles Darwin brought new species to light.

Tell the students that they are about to become scientific illustrators who will reveal to the world an entirely new species of fish, because they will invent it themselves. Ask them to choose whether it will be a cold-water or a tropical species. If it's a cold or temperate marine fish, does this fish swim in a school? Does it live on the bottom? Does it have to travel far?

If it's a coral reef fish, does it need to blend in with the reef environment? Does it have warning colors to let other fishes know it is dangerous or territorial? Would its shape, coloring, or skin mimic another kind of fish or other object (such as sea grass, coral, rock, and so on)? Does its body need to be shaped to be able to squeeze into coral crevices or tunnels? How else might it protect itself?

Once the learners have answered these questions, they can design and draw their fish, particularly if you provide a variety of field guides and reference books on fishes for youngsters to look through to get ideas. They may choose to give their fish both a scientific name and a common name that are descriptive of their animal. An organism's scientific name often describes some aspect of its appearance or behavior. As the discoverers, they may also choose to use their own name as part of the Latin name. Have them refer to field guides for examples of scientific names. Explain that each animal and plant species has its own scientific name that can be instantly recognized by naturalists around the world, whatever language they speak. This avoids the confusion of referring to an or-

ganism by its local common name and finding that a different animal altogether has the same name in a different part of the country or the world.

This system of scientific naming was created in the 1750s by a
Swedish naturalist, Carl van Linne (which is usually seen in its Latinized
version, Carolus Linneas). Each organism is assigned a genus name,
which is capitalized, and a species name in lower case. When it is written, it usually appears in italics or underlined. For example, the cod is
Gadus callarias. The sea creature with the claim to the longest name is the
green sea urchin: *Strongylocentrotus drobachiensis*. Ask students to compare
the length of their own names to this mouthful!

Coral Reefs

Who could blame a marine biologist or an underwater photographer
for preferring to explore the warm, crystalline waters of the tropics
over the frigid, murky northern seas? For whatever reason, there seem
to be many more books about coral reefs and their inhabitants than
there are about cold-water seas. Michael George's *Coral Reef* is a good
introduction with its outstanding close-up photographs of the coral
polyps that build the reef. It briefly explains what conditions reef-building corals need in order to grow and introduces us to some of the reef's
inhabitants.

Coral reefs are the creation of two principal architects: the coral
polyp and the zooxanthellae, single-celled plants living "under the skin"
of the coral animal. The coral polyp is a small vase-shaped creature about
the size of a pencil eraser that lives inside a stony house it builds itself. A
single opening takes in food and gets rid of wastes. This "mouth" is surrounded by a ring of tentacles. Inside are coiled, poison-tipped harpoons
called *nematocysts* that sting and paralyze prey.

The polyps could not build a reef without the help of their plant
companions, the zooxanthellae. The food and oxygen produced by the
plants are used by the polyp to help it grow. The zooxanthellae use the
wastes from the polyp—carbon dioxide and the nitrogen from the am-
monia—to help *them* grow. In addition, the zooxanthellae speed the
process by which the coral extracts calcium carbonate from sea water to
build its skeleton.

Many different species of corals make up a reef. Many have descriptive common names that conjure up a clear mental picture of what they
look like under the sea. Ask students to draw what these coral species
might look like: plate coral, brain coral, staghorn coral, finger coral, sea
fans, and sea whips. Find these in coral reef identification books or in
children's trade books. If they see an unfamiliar coral, challenge learners

to come up with their own descriptive names. After all, that's what scientists do!

Building your own coral reef

Students can make their own coral polyps. Cut a sheet of oak tag into a ring so that when it is taped together it resembles a volcano's cone. Leave a large enough opening so each child can poke her hand out through the top. This represents the coral's hard outer skeleton. Give each child a thin plastic glove (the kind kept in all school first-aid kits) and a yellow or green magic marker to apply dots to the glove, which will represent the zooxanthellae. This is the soft coral polyp. The children can put their gloved hand through the cone and wriggle their fingers to represent the feeding tentacles of the polyp. You may want to discuss how much bigger their polyps are than a real coral polyp.

Now students are ready to join a colony. Cut several X's about four or five inches long in some old sheets. Each sheet represents one colony of corals. Suspend the sheets between chairs or desks so children can crouch beneath them. Have several students gather under a sheet, one at each opening, with their coral polyp puppets. Explain that even though they are independent animals, they are all conected in a unit or colony. A colony of coral may be made up of thousands of individuals. Have each "colony" decide what kind of coral species it wants to be.

To demonstrate feeding behavior, pass out "plankton" (such as goldfish crackers or baby carrots) when students reach up through the sheet with their gloved hands. Like the polyps, the children need to pull their "tentacles" in to eat. You will be amazed by their aggressive feeding behavior, just like the real coral polyps!

Imagine the reaction in your community if a neighbor suddenly attacked, stabbed, and poisoned the household next door just because they were getting too close. On the reef it happens all the time. Two different species of corals may appear to live side by side peacefully by day. At night, the reef becomes a war zone as they compete in a life-and-death struggle for living space. When two coral colonies grow too close, one species attacks the other's coral polyps with their stinging nematocysts. White scars on dead coral mark where the attacks took place. The more aggressive species may eventually completely overgrow the losers. Scientists who have witnessed these coral wars report that different colonies of the *same* species of coral do not attack each other.

To make this clearer to students have them act it out. Set firm ground rules ahead of time being sure they understand that only a light tap on a neighboring coral by outermost polyps is permitted. Then have children predict which neighbors might become engaged in a battle for space. Ask, "Can colonies move away from each other?" In a crowded reef how do corals get more space? Who might attack whom? Remember, different colonies of the *same* species don't attack each other.

To help learners appreciate the complexity of a coral reef, fifth-grade teacher Doug Caldwell and art teacher Iona Desmond did a six-week afterschool project with third-grade students. The principal built frames for two five-foot-long coral reefs using a curved plywood base topped with chicken wire. The students patiently constructed the coral reef by bunching up paper towels soaked in a papier-mâché mix and stuffing them layer upon layer into the wire frame. Sea fans were cut from window screening. After the sculpture dried, the students painted the corals in a variety of electric colors. Then each child made a papier-mâché reef creature that he had researched using field guides supplied by a parent. Once these were painted, the animals were mounted on stiff wires (as from clothes hangers) or tucked in nooks and crannies throughout the reef.

A less time-consuming approach to building a classroom model of a reef is *Make Your Own Coral Reef* by Sue Wells. It provides all the materials to make a multilayered, three-dimensional punch-out model of a reef in admirable detail. Students who have created their own reef might enjoy reading how it is done professionally in two books by New England Aquarium staff: *Dive to the Coral Reefs* by Elizabeth Tayntor, Paul Erickson, and Les Kaufman, and *A Reef Comes to Life: Creating an Undersea Exhibit* by Nat Segaloff and Paul Erickson.

Reading about reefs

A variety of books such as *Coral Reefs* by Sylvia A. Johnson and *Look Closer: Coral Reef* by Barbara Taylor provide good overviews of reef life. The Great Barrier Reef has some of the most diverse reef populations in the world as witnessed by *A Walk on the Great Barrier Reef* by Caroline Arnold and *The Great Barrier Reef: A Treasure in the Sea* by Alice Thompson Gilbreath. Several of these books also explain about the different kinds of reefs: fringing (attached to the shoreline), barrier (separated from shore by a shallow lagoon), and atoll, a ring-shaped reef. Have students research their origins. Charles Darwin theorized that coral reefs in the Pacific Ocean built up along the sides of a volcanic island. As the island sank, the coral continued to grow upward until the volcanic cone disappeared altogether, creating an atoll. Have youngsters build models of each kind of reef from modeling clay.

Day shift and night shift on the reef

Ask students when they are most active: daytime or nighttime? Do they know people who work and play at night and sleep during the day? Songbirds (and most humans) wake with the day and return to roost at night. Bats erupt from caves and barns at nightfall to hunt for insects.

Mosquitoes buzz around in search of blood at dawn and at dusk. Each of us has a biological clock that tells us when to wake up and when to go to sleep.

To make room for all the residents of the densely populated reef, the coral reef community is divided into creatures of the day, the night, and the twilight. As one animal crawls out of its den, another prepares to take it over. The daytime crew depends mostly on sight and color to find or to avoid other residents of the reef. Nocturnal animals prowl a world without light, relying on their keen senses of smell, taste, and touch. In between day and night, large predators roam the reef, alert for weary commuters going home after a day of foraging or groggily waking up for a night on the town. Scientists estimate that one half to two thirds of all reef fishes are active by day. Another one quarter to one third sleep by day and hunt by night. Only ten percent of all reef species are most active at dawn and dusk. Mary Cerullo's *Coral Reef: A City That Never Sleeps* and Bill Sargent's *Night Reef: Dusk to Dawn on a Coral Reef* tell about which animals populate the day, night, and twilight reef.

Reef projects

Create a mural of twenty-four hours on the reef, with three different backgrounds: black construction paper for night, grey for dawn or dusk, and bright blue for daytime. Have learners research which animals are active during each period. Make an illustration or model of the animals and mount them on the most suitable part of the diurnal cycle, for example,

- Animals of the night: moray eel, octopus, brittle star, reef-building corals, spiny lobster, squirrelfish
- Twilight stalkers: sharks, jack, grouper, snapper
- Day shift: butterflyfish, clownfish, angelfish, parrotfish, surgeonfish, triggerfish, cleaner wrasse

Have students choose one coral reef animal and write a story about twenty-four hours in its life as if they were that animal. Have them think about these questions as they prepare their "autobiographies": When are you most active? Where do you go to rest? What do you eat? What eats you? How might you attract a mate or avoid predators? What problems or opportunities do you have in daylight, in twilight, at nighttime?

My favorite author of literature about the coral reef is Katherine Orr. Her books are both lyrical and factual, and her deep love of the Caribbean ecosystem and its culture shines through every colorful page. Orr's *Shelley* is the biography of a queen conch, an animal whose existence is now threatened in many places by shell collectors. *Leroy the Lob-*

ster is the tale of a Caribbean spiny lobster. Unlike American lobsters, spiny lobsters seem to tolerate each other's company and often share their dens in the coral reefs. They may alert other lobsters to danger by rubbing the base of their antennae against serrated ridges below their eyes to make loud rasping sounds.

Shelley and Leroy begin their lives as plankton, small, floating creatures. Their planktonic stages look totally unlike the adults they will become. Many forms of marine life start out as plankton. Using the illustrations in *Shelley* and from other sources, have students make up a game in which the players must match the planktonic stages of sea creatures like crabs, lobster, barnacles, fish, and queen conchs with their adult versions. Orr follows each animal through its life cycle, gently pointing out ways humans may exploit these animals.

Tropical seas are warm year-round. Temperate waters warm up in the summer but drop to nearly freezing in winter. Cold-water seas are never comfortable enough for swimming (at least for most of us humans). But where you will find *really* cold water is around the Antarctic continent. The Antarctic Ocean averages from just above freezing to just below freezing temperatures year-round.

The Frigid South: Antarctica

The Antarctic climate is too cold for almost all land animals. The average temperature on the Antarctic continent is –49°C. The lowest temperature ever recorded anywhere on earth was measured here at –128.6°F (–89°C). The water temperature averages a comparatively balmy 33°F or slightly colder. You'll find most of the life in Antarctica in or associated with the sea. Except for a few lichens and insects, most of the life in the Antarctic region has its roots in the sea. In *Summer Ice: Life Along the Antarctic Peninsula*, Bruce McMillan takes us on a photographic tour of the natural history of the Antarctic Peninsula. He fills the pages with images of krill, birds, seals, whales, algae, and marine mammals such as humpbacks, orcas, crabeater seals, Weddel seals, southern elephant seals, and Antarctic fur seals.

A layer of ice up to two miles thick covers a continent as big as the United States and Mexico combined. Frozen in the Antarctic ice is 70 percent of the world's fresh water and 90 percent of the world's ice. If it were divided up, every person on earth could have a chunk of ice larger than the Great Pyramid. Unlike the Arctic, there is some land underneath the ice cover.

When it's winter in the Northern Hemisphere, it's summer in Antarctica, but it's still mighty cold. Summer temperatures in coastal Antarctica hover around freezing while the South Pole rarely rises above 30°F below zero. It's so cold there that ice cream is stored outside and has to be microwaved before it can be eaten! It seems so forbidding, yet Antarctica holds a powerful attraction to explorers, scientists, and kids. Most visitors to Antarctica are researchers, but *Antarctic Encounter: Destination South Georgia* describes one family's journey around the Antarctic. In *A for Antarctica*, Jonathon Chester bounces between the natural history of the region and the people who study it with entries like *albatross, boots, crevasse, explorers, fossils*, and so on. This approach, though it uses hardly any words, gives the reader lots to think about. *Antarctica* by Helen Cowcher also provides an nice overview of the region.

Icebergs and glaciers

In *Icebergs and Glaciers*, Seymour Simon describes how glaciers and icebergs form. Since 98 percent of Antarctica is ice, and the Arctic is only ice (no land), it is an appropriate topic to introduce a study of the polar seas. *Danger—Icebergs!* by Roma Gans explains what these mountains of ice mean to sailors, how they are created, and how they disappear.

Let students experiment with ice cubes and chunks of snow and ice in a tub of water to compare how much of their forms sink below the water line. Like glaciers, icebergs in shallow water sometimes leave tracks of their movements in the muddy ocean floor. Use a ruler to measure how much of the "iceberg" is above water. How much is below? Why does ice float? (Because the water expands as the liquid changes to a solid, thus making it less dense.)

Add food coloring to water in another paper cup and stir. Freeze as before and float the ice cube in warm water in a clear bowl or small aquarium. Watch what happens when an iceberg drifts into warmer waters.

Ask students to speculate what happens to the salt in seawater when it freezes. Try an experiment of freezing salt water. Compare with an ice cube of fresh water. How do they taste?

We all know that water freezes at 0°C or 32°F. But is that always true? Fill four empty yogurt or cottage cheese containers, respectively, with fresh water, water with one tablespoon salt, two tablespoons of salt, and three tablespoons of salt. Have the children predict which container will freeze first and how long it will take, and record their predictions. Place the containers inside a refrigerator freezer or outdoors if it is cold enough. Take the temperature of each solution every fifteen minutes. Make a note of the time when each solution starts to freeze. Which freezes last? What temperature was it? Why doesn't the ocean freeze in most places? The seas around Antarctica tend to freeze around 28°F.

Ask students why road crews put salt on icy roads in winter. Design an experiment that shows that salt makes ice melt faster than just putting down sand or leaving the road untreated.

The Sea's Creatures

We have examined some of the places in the ocean where life flourishes and why (because there is light, food, and nutrients). Another way to approach a study of the ocean is to examine different groups of animals, such as birds (penguins), invertebrates or animals without backbones (lobsters), fishes (and particularly, sharks), and marine mammals (whales). Each group has evolved special adaptations that make it suitable for life in the sea.

Penguins

When you think of Antarctic animals, penguins immediately come to mind. They may look winsome, but a recent Antarctic visitor commented that these birds can be quite snappish. Who could blame them, sitting in cold, cramped rookeries on a barren landscape? There are a number of books about penguins, such as *Penguins* by Sylvia A. Johnson, Bruce McMillan's *Penguins at Home: Gentoos of Antarctica*, and *Looking at Penguins* by Dorothy Henshaw Patent.

Use a globe to point out that all seventeen species of penguins live south of the equator (and, consequently, a polar bear—a denizen of the northern hemisphere—and a penguin would only coexist in a zoo). Penguins live along the western and southern coasts of South America, the tip of Africa, southern Australia, New Zealand, the Galapagos Islands, and all around Antarctica. One species, the Galapagos penguin, lives on the equator in the path of the cold Peru Current. Seven different kinds of penguins visit Antarctica, but only two species, the Adelie and Emperor penguins, breed exclusively on the Antarctic continent.

Penguins, although birds, are designed for life in the sea. Some species spend as much as 75 percent of their lives at sea. They must come on land to lay their eggs and to raise their chicks. Heavy, solid bones act like a diver's weight belt, allowing them to stay submerged under water. Their wings shaped like flippers help them "fly under water" at speeds up to fifteen miles per hour. A streamlined body, paddlelike feet, insulating blubber, and watertight feathers all add to efficiency and comfort underwater. They also have a remarkable deep-diving ability.

In addition to blubber for insulating warmth, penguins have tightly packed feathers (up to seventy per square inch). Their stiff feathers overlap to provide waterproofing. They coat their feathers with oil from a gland near their tail to increase the impermeability. Their black-and-white coloring makes them nearly invisible to ocean predators. From below, the light belly blends in with the light surface of the water; from above, the dark back blends in with the dark depths of the ocean. This is called *countershading*. What other animals have countershading?

Penguins are the only birds that migrate by swimming. Magellanic penguins migrate up the west coast of South America to Tetas Point in northern Chile or up the east coast of South America past Argentina as far north as Rio de Janeiro in Brazil. Have youngsters draw their routes on a map of South America and estimate the distance they travel.

Like most birds, penguins have little or no sense of smell (a boon for anyone spending time in a crowded penguin rookery!). And their sense of taste is also limited, like other birds. Their vision appears to be better suited to water than air. Some scientists suspect they may be nearsighted on land.

On land, the penguin's color pattern helps regulate its body temperature. To find out how, lay a white piece of paper and a black piece of paper in the sun. Weight down the corners with small rocks. Let students put their hands against them to see that both pieces of paper are about the same temperature. Return in about half an hour and have them feel them again. Which one is warmer?

In their rookeries on land, penguins turn their black backs toward the sun to absorb its warmth and then face the sun when they want to cool down. They also frequently huddle together for warmth, taking turns being the outermost penguins.

Penguins are considered the most social of birds. Rookeries may contain millions of individuals. (As many as twenty-four *million* penguins visit the Antarctic continent!) Even at sea, they tend to swim and feed in groups. Many build nests, but the nests may be only a pile of rocks, scrapings, or hollows in the dirt. Emperor penguins build no nests; the males hold the egg on top of their feet under a loose fold of skin called the *brood patch*.

Brainstorm with learners ways that penguins are well adapted to cold water. Flying birds need a large wingspan to hold them up in the air, but small wings work best for birds swimming through the water. You can demonstrate this with two large sheets of paper. First, try to push a sheet of paper through a pan of water. It doesn't push very well. Then, fold another large sheet of paper five or six times and try pushing that through the water. The smaller, stiffer paper—like a penguin's wing—works better.

As a group, make a Venn diagram to show the ways that penguins are different from and similar to other birds. Then have different groups of students make Venn diagrams showing how penguins are similar and different from seals, whales, and fish. Using the ideas generated by a discussion about penguin adaptations and the Venn diagrams, have groups of children design a totally new marine animal that is also well adapted for the cold. Have them draw a picture of their new animal and have them explain the rationale behind the design of their animals and habitats.

Lobsters

As I learned researching *Lobsters: Gangsters of the Sea,* there are many kinds of lobsters: crayfish, slipper lobsters, and spiny lobsters. But for most connoisseurs, there is only one genuine lobster: the American lobster, *Homarus americanus.* It lives in waters off the coast from the Canadian Maritimes to North Carolina, but it is most abundant in the colder northern waters. The "American" lobster is a crustacean with a big-toothed *crusher* claw for pulverizing shells and a finer-edged *ripper* or *pincher* claw resembling a steak knife, for tearing soft flesh. (A lobster which carries its crusher claw on the right is a "right-handed" lobster.) It has eight walking legs. This arthropod also has small appendages around its mouth for gripping and shredding its food. Most books on lobsters have illustrations of the parts of a lobster. You can trace the outline to make a lobster puzzle for children to cut out and identify the parts: crusher claw, ripper or tearing claw, carapace, walking legs, antennae. (Or you can cook and eat a lobster and label its leftover parts!)

You can get a male and female lobster from the market and have children learn to distinguish the sexes by the first pair of feathery fins on the underside of the lobster, the *swimmerets.* They are hard on a male, soft on a female. *Lobsters Inside-Out: A Guide to the Maine Lobster* by Robert and Juanita Bayer also provides more information about the lobster's anatomy. Discover the *Lobster's Secret* by Kathleen Hollenbeck to learn more about the lobster's life cycle.

Trivia facts about lobsters abound. Perhaps you can suggest that students create posters or cartoons to illustrate some of these facts, such as

- Most lobsters weigh about a pound to a pound and a half when they are caught, but the largest lobster ever caught weighed over forty-four pounds.
- Lobsters can be cannibals.
- In the summer, the primary diet of lobsters is the lobster bait inside traps or thrown over the side of lobster boats. Some lobsters crawl into traps to eat and then escape afterward.
- You should never eat a green lobster. (It's still alive! A lobster turns red when it's cooked.)

Lobster catchers are as interesting as lobsters, and like them, tend to be a distinctive breed. Their lives are depicted in various ways in *Going Lobstering* by Jerry Pallotta, *Finest Kind O'Day: Lobstering in Maine* by Bruce McMillan, *Lobsterman* by Dahlov Ipcar, and in *Lobsters: Gangsters of the Sea*. Lobstermen have a language all their own. Stump your students with lobster riddles and with vocabulary words drawn from the trade books, such as

When is a lobster a *chicken*? . . . (When it weighs about one pound.)

When is a lobster a *pistol*? . . . (When it has no claws.)

Why wouldn't a lobsterman with *shorts* want to meet a marine patrol officer? . . . (He has lobsters that don't meet the legal size.)

Why shouldn't a lobster walk into the *kitchen*? . . . (It's the first chamber of a lobster trap.)

Your students can pretend they are a lobster gang (as the harvesters from the same harbor or port are called). Have each child decide how many traps she will fish (at 50 dollars apiece). Have each plot her territory on a map of the coast. Make a circle around fishing areas that claim part of the ocean floor. (This division remains unspoken but understood in lobstering society.) How large an area do they think they can cover in a seven-hour workday moving at about 10-20 mph? Lobster catchers may earn about three dollars for every lobster sold to a lobster pound. How does that compare to what the consumer pays? Have students check on the current price of lobster at the supermarket and at restaurants. Assuming they catch an average of two lobsters per trap per day, how long will it take to pay off the cost of their traps? What is the lobster catcher's hourly wage? What other expenses does a lobster catcher incur (boat, winch, license, fuel, lobster gauge, bait, barrels, rubber bands for claws, other gear)? What does a lobster catcher have to do after lobstering all day? (Sell lobsters, fix traps, buy more bait and gas, refill bait bags, and so on.)

If you have traps, you need buoys in order to find them again. Buoys are usually attached to either end of a string of traps. A string can hold up to forty traps, but fifteen or twenty are more common. Have each child decide on the colors for his buoys. You can construct a lobster buoy by taping an empty toilet paper roll to the mouth of an empty half-gallon plastic milk jug. To make the paint stick to the plastic, try mixing a little liquid detergent with the tempera paint. Make a classroom key that matches buoys and lobster harvesters.

If you live in a coastal community, you could culminate the unit by inviting a lobster harvester and a marine patrol officer to class to show their gear and discuss lobster conservation. In some places, the state fisheries agency will donate confiscated lobster traps and buoys to teachers to use for educational purposes.

Fishes

Ask students, "What makes a fish a fish?" You can make a list of their responses and direct them to books such as *What Is a Fish?* by Robert Snedden to check their responses. By the end of their study their list of characteristics of a fish may include: lives in water, has gills for breathing, has fins for swimming, has a lateral line running down the length of its body to sense underwater vibrations of other fish in its school, often has a balloon-shaped swim bladder that keeps it at desired level in the ocean, can't blink (because it doesn't have eyelids), and is cold-blooded (its body takes on the temperature of the water around it).

With more than twenty thousand species of fish in the world, it's hard to describe a typical fish. There are advantages to the odd adaptations many fishes have, as *Big Al* by Andrew Clemens proves. Big Al is a monstrous-looking fish that just wants to belong. Thanks to his looks, sweet-natured but ugly Big Al saves a school of fish.

Try to keep some fish in the classroom, even for a few days. Students can observe and record how the fish move, breathe, and how they use their various fins. You might help them notice that top and bottom fins provide stability to keep the fish upright, side fins are used for turning and stopping, and the tail fin propels the fish forward.

Japanese fish printing, *gyotaku*, was reportedly invented as a way for Japanese fishermen to preserve the beauty of their catch before selling it at market. Buy a fresh fish, one with clear eyes and no smell. Flounders and other flat fish work particularly well. Wash the fish with soap and water to remove the slime that protects a fish's skin. Pat dry and lay the fish on newspaper. Spread the fins and hold them open by placing PlayDoh underneath them. Using tempera paint or diluted linoleum paint, lightly paint the entire body. Lay a piece of newsprint paper on top of the fish. Holding the paper in place with one hand, rub your other hand down the length of the fish's body making sure to include all the fins and the eye(s). (I tell students to give the fish a back rub.) Gently lift the paper and repeat with a clean sheet of paper before repainting the fish. Usually the second print shows better detail. The same fish can be used by many students. Ask students to identify the parts of a fish—fins, gill covering, lateral line, eyes, scales—on their fish print.

When humans enter the water they have to take on some of the characteristics of fishes. Invite a scuba diver into class to demonstrate how scuba (Self-Contained Underwater Breathing Apparatus) works. Ask students, "How does a diver become like a fish?"

FISH	DIVER
gills	scuba tank
scales	wetsuit
fins	flippers
bulbous eyes	face mask
swimbladder	inflatable vest and weight belt

Ask students to list ways that fishes protect themselves and someone will inevitably answer, "Schooling." Schooling also makes finding food and mates easier. *Swimmy* by Leo Lionni is a classic tale that affirms the advantages of schooling. To describe how fish orient themselves in a school, have students stand outside on a windy day and close their eyes. Ask them to point toward the direction from which the wind is blowing. Like wind against our faces, fish perceive the movements of others in their school by sensing vibrations against their lateral line.

Sharks

I started off my book, *Sharks: Challengers of the Deep,* with a quiz of true or false statements:

Sharks have no bones.	T	F
Sharks sink when they stop swimming.	T	F
Sharks rarely lose their teeth.	T	F
Sharks can not live in fresh water.	T	F
Sharks are not fish.	T	F
Sharks eat each other.	T	F
More people are killed by bee stings than by shark attacks.	T	F
Sharks may help us find a cure for cancer.	T	F

Kids invariably get high scores on the quiz because almost everyone under the age of twelve is an expert on sharks. Publishers appreciate this fact, too, as you can tell from the plethora of children's books about sharks (matched closely by books on dinosaurs and whales).

Capitalizing on that passion, there are any number of good books on sharks, including Ruth Berman's *Sharks,* Eyewitness Books' *Shark* by Miranda Macquitty, and *Sharks!* by June Behrens. To my mind, one of the stand-out books done, like those in the Eyewitness series, is *Sharks: Great Creatures of the Sea* published in Australia and distributed in the United States by Children's Press. It is jam-packed with information about shark species, shark attacks, sharks in legends, films, and literature, and so forth, laid out in a news magazine format. Not much text, but closer-than-you'd-ever-want-to-get photos distinguish the *World of Nature Sharks* by Lee Server.

You might launch a study of sharks by asking students to compare them to other fishes. They are unlike bony fishes in that they have a skeleton of cartilage (like in our ears) instead of bone, five to seven gill slits on each side instead of a single gill covering, many rows of teeth, and no swimbladder.

As hard as it is to generalize about fishes, it's even harder to find a "typical" shark among the 350 or so different species of sharks, skates, and rays. You could use this story to explain some of the characerics and behaviors typical of most species:

A DAY IN THE LIFE OF A SHARK

As always, Sharp Fin was alert and patrolling her territory early, just before dawn. Occasionally her rigid dorsal fin sliced through the surface of the water, leaving barely a ripple in its wake. She was graceful and lean, as streamlined as a torpedo. Before long the rising sun shot long shafts of light deep into the clear water, creating alternating patches of light and shadows. Sharp Fin knew what lurked in every shadow of the coral reef. Her finely tuned senses recognized most movements immediately. Nothing unusual caught her attention this morning. This day would be like every other day—almost.

Sharp Fin was a typical shark, if there is such a thing. She was about four feet long with a grey back fading to white underneath. From below, her white belly helped her blend in with the sunlit surface waters; from above, her dark back was indistinguishable from the shadowy depths. This countershading helped her to avoid being seen by predators. Not that she had many predators now. When she was younger, she had been chased by seals and sea lions. Now that she was full-grown, her only enemies were other sharks and humans. She had managed to reach ten years with only a few scars on her tough hide to mark her narrow escapes from predators and the loving attentions of male sharks.

Some sense within her had drawn her back to her place of birth. It was as if she were part of the earth's magnetic field. She could feel its influence guiding her to where she had been before. Here, several years earlier, Sharp Fin had been born alive, not hatched from an egg like most fishes. She had had to flee immediately so her mother or other sharks wouldn't eat her.

Now the shallow reef was safe—at least for her.

Ever since her birth, Sharp Fin had been swimming continuously, pushing water through her five gill slits to feed oxygen to her body. Spiracles, openings near her nose, filtered more oxygenated water to help supply her heart and small brain.

A school of silvery fish passed above her. She sprang at them with a burst of speed, but they sensed her approach against their lateral lines. All scattered before her open jaws, except one. It had already lost its top fin to disease. Its other fins were coated with white and frayed at the edges. The silver fish was just too sick to escape its fate. Sharp Fin swallowed it whole.

Her strong digestive juices would soon convert her meal into usuable energy. Although the fish wasn't large, it would be enough to keep her going for days. She could go months without eating, if necessary, drawing upon the oil reserves stored in her liver.

Sharp Fin ate anything she could catch easily—many kinds of fish, including eels, stingrays, and smaller sharks, as well as octopus, crabs, shrimp, occasionally a small sea turtle or a bird that lingered too long on the water's surface. She even ate lowly worms if it came to that. She preferred attacking old or sick animals because they were so easy to catch. She never caught their disease. In fact, she never got sick, ever. Only old age, however long away that may be, or a predator, could end her life. Rather it was she, the shark, which was known in this region as "the bringer of the end."

She spied the hull of a fishing boat glide overhead. She started to follow it, aware that in the past it had brought her wounded, struggling fish that she had easily snatched before the fishermen could haul them out of the water. She saw a large fish dangling on a line behind the boat. She rushed at it and tried to tear it away, but instead she became hooked! She thrashed violently. Sharp Fin finally managed to break away, but she was bleeding from her mouth and gills. No matter, she didn't seem bothered by pain.

In seconds, five other sharks appeared from nowhere. They rushed at Sharp Fin, devoured her in a few crescent-shaped bites, and then turned their fury on each other. Out of control, they spun around and around, snapping at anything in the water, even the boat. The fishermen clung to their small craft, terrified that the sharks would smash a hole in the side. They were certain that the sharks had come for them.

After about ten minutes the frenzy ended as quickly as it had begun. The sharks disappeared. The water was calm and clear again. Not a trace of the sharks remained.

The fishermen rowed to shore and hauled their boat high onto the beach. They hugged their waiting families tightly, happy to be alive.

They dug out the teeth of Shark Fin's predators from the hull. They waved these before the crowd that gathered at the shore to prove that they had been attacked by sharks.

After reading this story, you can ask students, "What are the characteristics of the 'typical' shark? What is the behavior of a typical shark? What enemies do sharks have? Who did you feel sympathy for in this story?" Have them research a specific species of shark and write a day-in-the-life-of biography about it. Or have students write two stories about an encounter between a human and a shark, first from the shark's perspective and then from the human's perspective.

One aspect of shark research that grabs most people is the subject of shark attacks. Over the years, most attempts to protect humans from shark attacks have met with marginal success at best. Have students research the effectiveness of chemical shark repellents (like the Shark Chaser used in World War II by downed pilots), shark cages, nets and bubble barriers across swimming beaches, a chain-link dive suit, the Johnson shark screen (basically a floating plastic bag that insulates the person's shape and smell from the water), the bang stick, a shark billy, wearing dark colors, and any other defenses against shark attacks they can find. Based on their research, have teams of learners design their own antishark protection.

Most shark books feature a rogue's gallery of man-eating sharks. Ask students, "If you were diving in the ocean and met a shark, which species would you hope it would be? Which would you rather it were not?"

Whales

As with sharks, children are natural authorities on whales. It might be useful to ask students to make a list of what they know, what they want to know, and what they learned for this unit. They may be surprised to find out that, for instance, whales do not spray water from their blowholes when they spout (the spray is from water trapped at the opening of the blowhole), or that whales evolved from land animals. Fiction books like *Amos and Boris* by William Steig or *Burt Dow: Deep-Water Man* by Robert McCloskey might be a good way to start talking about whales, followed by reading introductory nonfiction books such as *Whales: The Gentle Giants* by Joyce Milton.

Whales are mammals, like we are. They are warm-blooded, nurse their young, and breathe air. To demonstrate how blubber can serve as insulation, use solid shortening to substitute for the thick blubber that insulates warm-blooded whales from the cold sea. You will need four large, resealable plastic bags; one pound of solid vegetable shortening; a bucket of cold water with ice cubes or snow; a watch with a second hand or a stopwatch. Spoon solid shortening into one bag. Have a volunteer put her hand inside another bag, and then insert that hand into the bag with the shortening. Knead the shortening to make sure the hand is completely surrounded by shortening. Then have the volunteer cover the other hand with two plastic bags (without any shortening). This is the "control" for your experiment. Have the child place both hands into a bucket of ice cold water. Time how long she can keep each hand under water.

Next you can challenge your students to breathe like a whale: Lie on the floor on your back. Blow out all the air you can from your lungs, then take a deep breath and hold it as long as you can. Blow out quickly and repeat. What was the longest anyone could hold their breath? Compare that time to a sperm whale, which can hold its breath for up to an hour.

Eating like a whale

There are two groups of whales: toothed whales and baleen whales. This activity allows students to imitate their feeding mechanisms to see what kind of prey each group targets. Baleen whales ("moustached whales") have plates of baleen hanging like broom bristles from their upper jaws that sieve plankton, krill, and small fish from seawater. Baleen is made of the same material as our fingernails. The whale uses its flabby tongue to squeeze water through the baleen and lick off the plankton. Ten species of whales are baleen whales, including the largest animal that ever lived, the blue whale. The right whale, humpback whale, fin whale, minke whale, and sei whale are all baleen whales.

Toothed whales don't chew their food; they use their teeth only to grasp their prey: fish, squid, and in some cases, other marine mammals. Toothed whales include sperm whales—Moby Dick was one—orca or killer whales, pilot whales, narwhals, and dolphins. Cynthia Rylant's *The Whales* depicts different species of whales through bright splashes of color and almost childlike paintings. A key in the back explains what species each one painting represents.

Challenge students to eat like a whale. Have them use tools to simulate eating with baleen and with teeth. Sprinkle parsley flakes (for krill) and fish crackers or raisins (to represent fish) into a large pan of water. Explain that different kinds of whales eat different kinds of food. Some eat fish such as herring, capelin, or cod, and others feed on krill, a shrimp-like creature which occurs in huge pink concentrations in Antarctica. Baleen and toothed whales have different adaptations that enable them to catch their preferred prey. Let students experiment with the tongs and the comb to see which kind of prey each harvests more efficiently. Discuss which tool represents toothed whales (tongs) and which represents baleen whales (comb). Is baleen more effective at picking up krill or fish? Why? Which food does teeth work better for? A medium-sized blue whale weighing one hundred tons may eat up to four tons of krill a day. What does this suggest about the efficiency of baleen as a feeding mechanism?

Whales depend on sonar to help them travel long distances, avoid objects, and find food. You can demonstrate how sonar works by placing a glass pie plate filled with water onto an overhead projector so that the image of the water projects onto a screen. Drop one drop of water from an eyedropper into the middle of the pie plate from a height of about six to twelve inches above the plate. This will create a wave that radiates outward from the middle of the plate and bounces back from the sides to simulate how sonar reflects sound waves back from objects.

Sonar and sound are imporant part of whales' survival and communication. Dyan Sheldon writes in *The Whales' Song* about a little girl whose grandmother tells her stories about the whales' songs. One moonlit night she watches by the bay and hears the songs herself. You can play whale songs for the class. Humpback whales are noted for their songs that can last for hours and be hear over vast distances. Over twenty years ago, Roger Payne began to record and diagram the complexity of the songs of humpback whales. His *Songs of the Humpback Whale* is still available, and musicians such as Judy Collins and the Paul Winter Consort have incorporated whale songs into their recordings.

Whale watching

Whale watching has inspired some outstanding books, both fiction and nonfiction. At the simplest level, Bruce McMillan's *Going on a Whale Watch* features photographs of whale behavior with two-word descriptions such as *lunge feeding* or *deep dive*. Nonetheless, there is a wealth of information here for all students. It is the only book I've seen that illustrates what the whale looks like below the surface at the same time as you see whale behavior at the surface. In addition, a "visual glossary" at the back of the book provides more details about breaching, feeding, and diving behavior, as well information on whale species and whale anatomy. John Waters's *Watching Whales* gives the history of whale watching and takes us on a whale watch with a fifth-grade class. Stories with a whale-watch setting include *I Wonder If I'll See a Whale* by Frances Ward Weller and *Nobody Listens to Me* by Leslie Guccione, a book about young girl who is worried that her dad's whale-watching business may be harming the whales.

Ask students if they have ever been on a whale watch. What do they imagine it would be like? How do whale watchers and scientists identify individual whales? Whale watchers give each whale an identification number and a name that describes some physical characteristic or marking—patterns on their tail flukes, scars, shape of back fins. Researchers catalog and name whales and track them for years on both their feeding and breeding grounds.

The tail fluke of a humpback is like a fingerprint. Create a template of a whale fluke for the class. Tell class members that they may "adopt" a whale and design their own black-and-white fluke markings to identify it. Have them name their whales. Make a class whale-watching guide using the fluke patterns and distribute copies of each fluke pattern to the members of the class. See if other students can identify the whales by their tails.

When a whale pulls up alongside a whale-watching boat, you can really appreciate how big it is. According to *Going on a Whale Watch*, minke whales can grow as large as thirty-five feet, humpbacks up to fifty-five feet, and finback whales as long as eighty feet. Mark off a rope in ten-foot increments and have children measure off the length of these whales in the school parking lot to give them a better sense of the animals' size. Why can whales grow so large in the sea? Buoyancy—one of the benefits of ocean living!

Books about individual whales include *Crystal: The Story of a Real Baby Whale* by Karen Smyth. Crystal is a baby humpback born to its mother, Salt, on Silver Bank just north of the Dominican Republic. We learn how Crystal eats, grows, and migrates across the North Atlantic between Silver Bank and Stellwagen Bank, off Massachusetts. The Latin name of the humpback whale is *Megaptera novaeangliae*, which means "big-winged New Englander." It is known for its spectacular leaps and long white side flippers. After giving birth during the winter or early spring, mothers bring their calves to the rich feeding grounds of New England in the North Atlantic.

Discuss why whales migrate such long distances. Ask, "What dangers do whales face during their migration?" On a chart of the western Atlantic Ocean, have students mark the two ends of the humpback's annual migration between Stellwagen Bank and Silver Bank.

You can have teams of students create a board game of whale migration using a map of the Atlantic Ocean or Pacific Ocean, depending on the species, as the game board. Have them make up chance cards that show the hazards and benefits along the way. *Crystal* describes many of the dangers, as does *Ibis: A True Whale Story*. John Himmelman recounts how Ibis, a female humpback, was found seriously tangled in a gill net, with barely enough strength to surface to breathe. Her rescue was celebrated as a rare instance when a whale was saved from entanglement.

Watching over whales

One way students can help monitor and protect whales is by joining WhaleNet, a project to track whales. Student researchers share their sightings at http://www.whale.wheelock.edu on the World Wide Web. Or they could raise money to adopt a whale through the following organizations:

Whale Adoption Project, P.O. Box 388, North Falmouth, Massachusetts 02556

New England Aquarium, Central Wharf, Boston, Massachusetts 02110

College of the Atlantic, 105 Eden Street, Bar Harbor, Maine 04609

Protect a Pod, P. O. Box 1577, Friday Harbor, Washington 98250

Mingan Island Cetacean Study, 285 Green Street, Lambert, Quebec J4P1T3, Canada

Contributions fund research, and generally "foster parents" receive a photo and background information on "their" whale.

Sometimes whales, like humans, take a wrong turn that can get them into trouble, as in *The Whale in Lowell's Cove* by Jane W. Robinson and *Humphrey, The Wayward Whale* by Ernest Callenbach and Christine Leefeldt. With human help, their stories can have a happy ending. In *The Whale in Lowell's Cove*, a young humpback swims into a bay along the coast of Maine probably in pursuit of a school of pogies (menhaden). She becomes trapped behind a seine net set up to round up the pogies. Fishermen and whale experts devise a plan to keep the pogies and free the whale so she can migrate down the coast before winter. Humphrey, another young humpback, enters San Francisco Bay and swims seventy miles up river until the water is so shallow he scrapes his long fins on the bottom. Scientists play underwater recordings of whale sounds to lure him back to sea. Both are true stories.

Ask students to write their own whale rescue stories. They may want to contact staff and volunteers of whale rescue networks through major aquariums, state fisheries agencies, or research centers to request background information about the Marine Mammal Stranding Network. Or invite students to write a whale of a tale by

- Chronicling the travels of a mother whale migrating between the cold waters where it feeds in summer and the tropics where it gives birth.

- Witnessing the birth of a baby whale as a member of a pod.

- Imagining how whales communicate with each other.

- Pretending you are a scientist who could interview a whale directly. What kind of questions would you ask?

- Imagining you are in a small inflatable boat called a Zodiac. You have placed yourself between and mother whale and a whaling ship whose harpoon is aimed directly in your path.

People and the Sea

You could begin or end a study of the oceans with a unit on people and the sea—ocean explorers, heroes, and villains. People through the ages have earned their living from the sea or have been drawn to its mystery and promise. Ask learners to make a list of how people have used the oceans. Label the ways as being *good, bad,* or *makes no difference* to the ocean. This list will inevitably lead to a discussion of how people have abused and protected the ocean. Almost any ocean book worth its salt deals at least in passing with these issues nowadays.

People have been exploring the sea ever since they started building boats, but two modern-day explorers you might profile are Sylvia Earle, who holds the world record for the deepest solo dive, and Robert Ballard, who discovered the *Titanic* and the *Bismarck*. He was also one of the first scientists to study the deep-sea vents. Dr. Earle's exploits are described in *Window on the Deep: The Adventures of Underwater Explorer Sylvia Earle* by Andrea Conley. *Deep-Sea Vents: Living Worlds Without Sun* by John F. Waters describes what scientists like Ballard have seen from tiny submarines several miles below the ocean's surface. Dr. Ballard wrote about his expeditions to locate sunken history in *The Discovery of the* Titanic, *Exploring the* Titanic, and *Exploring the* Bismarck. Titanic *Lost and Found* by Judy Donnelly documents the sinking and discovery for younger readers. Several books capture the elegance and tragedy of the maiden voyage of the Titanic: *On Board the* Titanic by Shelley Tanaka, the true story of passenger Jack Thayer's harrowing night atop an overturned lifeboat, and *Polar the Titanic Bear* by Daisy Spedden, about a teddy bear belonging to one of the young passengers.

When Bob Ballard first found the *Titanic* in 1985, he refused to release its coordinates so treasure hunters couldn't plunder the grave of 1,500 people (which they have since done). Later, Ballard revealed that the ship was lying over two miles deep at coordinates 41°43′N, 49°56′W. Use these coordinates to locate the *Titanic's* resting place on a globe and to explain the importance of latitude and longitude to navigation. Challenge students to find the latitude and longitude of their own town. Trace the maiden voyage's proposed route from Southhampton, England, to New York Harbor. Another view of salvaging sunken ships is provided by Gail Gibbons's *Sunken Treasure*, which documents the discovery of the Spanish galleon *Atocha*.

Abbie Burgess is a heroine you may want to highlight. When her lighthouse keeper father was trapped onshore by a tremendous winter storm in 1856, this brave girl tended the lighthouse for a month while caring for her sick mother and her family. Her true story is detailed in *Keep the Lights Burning, Abbie* by Peter and Connie Roop and in *The Original Biography of Abbie Burgess, Lighthouse Heroine* by Dorothy Holder Jones and Ruth Sexton Sargent.

Fairy Tales of the Sea

Any study of the literature of the oceans would be incomplete without some tales of sailors' superstitions, legends, and folklore of the sea. Ask students to research stories about mermaids, selkies, sea monsters, and the Bermuda Triangle. Stories that can start them off are *The Mermaid and the Whale* by Georgess McHargue, a retelling of a sailors' tale about a mermaid off Cape Cod who falls in love with a whale, and *Greyling* by Jane Yolen, a myth about a Scottish selkie, a seal that takes human form. *Monster Myths: The Truth About Water Monsters* by Staton Rabin will give them the low-down on sea monsters.

Ask learners to draw a picture of a mermaid. Explain that sailors may have mistaken the sea cow or manatee for a mermaid, possibly because the mother nurses her young at the surface of the sea. Christopher Columbus claimed to have seen three mermaids on a voyage to the New World in 1493. He wrote in his log, "They are not so beautiful as they are painted."

Ask students to describe how a mermaid is like a mammal. (Mammal characteristics: breathe air through lungs, give birth to live babies, nurse their young, have hair or fur, are warm-blooded.) How are mermaids like fish? (Refer back to fish characteristics on page 129.) To compare their mermaid to the real thing, students might want to read *The Vanishing Manatee* by Margaret Goff Clark.

The mermaid legend extends to the beach. You can ask students how objects like the jingle shell got the nickname, *mermaid's toenail*, how the skate egg case became a *mermaid's purse*, and why the razor clam is known as *merman's razor*. You can have class members create a fairy tale about mermaids and mermen, using *Mermaid in a Tidal Pool* or Hans Christian Anderson's *The Little Mermaid* (remodeled for a new generation by Walt Disney Productions).

Nightmares of the Sea: Oil Spills

Not all of our images of the ocean are so romantic. In fact, many people have an image of the ocean as an environment in trouble. A 1996 national public opinion survey indicated that 81 percent of Americans believe that oil spill accidents are a very serious problem and that they account for the majority of the ocean's pollution, according to a survey conducted by the Marine Conservation Initiative in June 1996. Whether or not this perception is accurate, 3.25 million tons of oil enter the world's oceans each year, making it an issue worth addressing in class. Oil tankers transport millions of gallons of oil around the globe. If there is a leak or oil spill while these giant tankers are unloading or while the ships are navigating through the narrow channels or inside harbors, oil may wash up on the shores of a bay where it becomes trapped and coats everything—shoreline, plants, marine mammals, and birds.

Many different methods are used to clean up oil spills. Some materials absorb the oil; some make the oil disperse or settle to the bottom; some, such as oil booms, contain the oil until it can be suctioned up with hoses and removed. Read *Spill! The Story of the* Exxon Valdez by Terry Carr to see how people worked to clean up a major spill of nearly eleven million gallons. In *Oil Spill!*, a Let's-Read-and-Find-Out Science Book, Melvin Berger explains that eleven million gallons would fill over one thousand large swimming pools, giving children a way to relate to the size of the spill.

Thick oil can smother animals like birds and sea otters. It clogs the feeding and breathing mechanisms of filter feeders like barnacles and clams. If swallowed, it can poison animals. Over the long term, oil can cause cancer in marine life. *Sea Otter Rescue: The Aftermath of an Oil Spill* by Roland Smith is a firsthand report of how volunteers captured, cleaned, and monitored the health of sea otters coated with oil by the *Exxon Valdez* spill.

Birds are also damaged by oil spills when they land on the surface of the water. Ask students to examine a bird feather. What do birds use their feather for? (Keeping dry and warm.) The learners may feel some oiliness on the feather, which allows the feather to resist becoming waterlogged. Notice how it can fluff up after you handle it. Drop it into a pan of clean water. Does it float? Shake it off. Allow it to dry completely. Does it still fluff up?

Cleaning up a spill

To learn more about the effects of an oil spill, have students drop a bird feather into a pan of water and oil. What happens to it? Have them try to clean it. Some students may use liquid detergent; others may just scrub with a toothbrush. Allow the feather to dry, or dry it with a hair dryer. Does it still fluff up? Drop it into a pan of water. Does it still float as well as before? This gives you some indication that the feather has lost its ability to insulate (by trapping air) as well as to resist water.

How are oil spills cleaned up? Melvin Berger's *Oil Spill!* describe many cleanup techniques in a simple, well-illustrated manner. Help your youngsters learn about an oil spill by constructing a classroom model. Pour cooking oil into several large glass pans set up at different stations to represent an oil spill in the harbor. Ask students, "Where does the oil congregate?" (It floats on the surface.) "What happens to an object (you can use a cork) that you drop into the water?" (It becomes coated with oil.)

Put some of the oil mixture in a glass bottle filled with water. Put on the cap and shake the bottle vigorously (like in a storm or wave action). What happens to the oil? (Some of it mixes with the water.) After a time, some of the oil will evaporate, some will sink to the bottom, and some will come onshore. Have students consider what would happen to organisms that floated on the surface (sea birds, ducks, seaweeds, planktonic animals), that need to come to the surface to breathe (whales, seals, sea turtles), or that live on the bottom (flounders, sea urchins, lobsters, crabs)?

Divide the students into oil spill cleanup teams whose job it is to clean up the mess of the classroom spill. Have them try several materials and record how well each one works. Have available: cotton balls, hay, cut-up panty hose, aquarium nets, paper towels, popcorn, sponges, sawdust, sand, bandage pads, drinking straws, rope, string, turkey basters or eyedroppers, popsicle sticks, and liquid dishwashing detergent diluted in a spray bottle of water. Let each team of students choose several different materials to test. Then have the students make up a plan for how they will use each material and have them test it.

Afterward, discuss how well their efforts worked. Was all the oil removed? How well might their methods work on an actual spill? Discuss what kind of equipment actual oil spill cleanup personnel use and how it correlates to items they used (oil containment boom, skimmer, dispersants, oil sorbent material, and so forth).

As in *Oil Spill!*, you might end this project by discussing ways to prevent oil spills. As Melvin Berger points out in this primary-level book, children can write to their Congressional representatives to lobby for effective environmental protection.

Underwater explorer Sylvia Earle is frequently asked to name the greatest threat to the world's oceans. In her book, *Sea Change*, she writes, "If I had to name the single most frightening and dangerous threat to the health of the oceans, the one that stands alone is *ignorance*: lack of understanding, a failure to relate our destiny to that of the sea, or to make connections between the health of the coral reefs and our own health, between the fate of the great whales and the future of humankind." These connections are what environmental science is all about. Whether as a researcher, an armchair explorer, or a fourth-grade student, our task is the same: to understand and preserve these connections. Sylvia Earle urges, "This is the time as never before and perhaps never again to establish policies—on a small personal scale as well as a broad public scale—to protect and maintain planetary health"(Earle 1995, 2).

Children's Books Cited

ADRIAN, MARY. 1972. *A Day and a Night in a Tidepool.* New York: Hastings House.

ANDERSEN, HANS CHRISTIAN. 1971. *The Little Mermaid.* Translated by Eva LeGallienne. New York: Harper & Row.

ARNOLD, CAROLINE. 1988. *A Walk on the Great Barrier Reef.* Minneapolis, MN: Carolrhoda Books.

BALLARD, ROBERT. 1990. *The Discovery of the* Titanic. Avenal, NJ: Random House Value Publishing.

———. 1991. *Exploring the* Bismarck. New York: Scholastic.

———. 1991. *Exploring the* Titanic. New York: Scholastic.

BANNAN, JAN. 1989. *Sand Dunes.* Minneapolis, MN: Carolrhoda Books.

BAYER, ROBERT, and JUANITA BAYER. 1989. *Lobsters Inside-Out: A Guide to the Maine Lobster.* Bar Harbor, ME: Acadia Publishing Co.

BEHRENS, JUNE. 1990. *Sharks!* Chicago: Children's Press

BENDICK, JEANNE. 1992. *Exploring an Ocean Tide Pool.* New York: Henry Holt Books for Young Readers.

BERGER, MELVIN. 1994. *Oil Spill!* New York: HarperCollins Children's Books.

BERMAN, RUTH. 1995. *Sharks.* Minneapolis, MN: Carolrhoda Books.

BOWDEN, JOAN CHASE. 1979. *Why the Tides Ebb and Flow.* Boston: Houghton Mifflin.

CALLENBACH, ERNEST, and CHRISTINE LEEFELDT. 1986. *Humphrey, The Wayward Whale.* Berkeley, CA: Heyday Books.

Carle, Eric. 1991. *A House for Hermit Crab*. Boston: Picture Book Studio, Ltd.

Carpenter, Mimi. 1981. *What the Sea Left Behind*. Camden, ME: Down East Books.

———. 1985. *Mermaid in a Tidal Pool*. Oakland, ME: Beachcomber Press.

Carr, Terry. 1991. *Spill! The Story of the* Exxon Valdez. New York: Franklin Watts.

Cerullo, Mary. 1993. *Sharks: Challengers of the Deep*. New York: Cobblehill Books.

———. 1994. *Lobsters: Gangsters of the Sea*. New York: Cobblehill Books.

———. 1996. *Coral Reef: A City That Never Sleeps*. New York: Cobblehill Books.

Chester, Jonathon. 1995. *A for Antarctica*. Berkeley, CA: Tricycle Press.

Clark, Margaret Goff. 1990. *The Vanishing Manatee*. New York: Cobblehill Books.

Clemens, Andrew. 1991. *Big Al*. New York: Scholastic.

Cole, Joanna. 1992. *The Magic School Bus on the Ocean Floor*. New York: Scholastic.

Cole, Sheila. 1985. *When the Tide Is Low*. New York: Lothrop, Lee & Shepard Books.

Conley, Andrea. 1991. *Window on the Deep: The Adventures of Underwater Explorer Sylvia Earle*. New York: Franklin Watts.

Coulombe, Deborah A. 1984. *The Seaside Naturalist*. Englewood Cliffs, NJ: Prentice Hall.

Coupe, S., and R. Coupe. 1990. *Sharks: Great Creatures of the Sea*. Chicago: Children's Press.

Cowcher, Helen. 1990. *Antarctica*. New York: Farrar, Straus & Giroux.

Dethier, Vincent. 1981. *Newberry: The Life and Times of a Maine Clam*. Camden, ME: Down East Books.

Donnelly, Judy. 1987. Titanic *Lost and Found*. New York: Random House Books for Young Readers.

Doubilet, Anne, and David Doubilet. 1991. *Under the Sea from A to Z*. New York: Crown Books for Young Readers.

Epstein, Sam, and Beryl Epstein. 1985. *What's for Lunch? The Eating Habits of Seashore Creatures*. New York: Macmillan Children's Books.

Gans, Roma. 1987. *Danger—Icebergs!* New York: Harper Trophy.

GARLAND, SHERRY. 1995. *The Summer Sands.* San Diego: Gulliver Books.

GEORGE, MICHAEL. 1992. *Coral Reef.* Mankato, MN: Creative Education.

GIBBONS, GAIL. 1988. *Sunken Treasure.* New York: HarperCollins Children's Books.

———. 1991. *Surrounded by Sea: Life on a New England Fishing Island.* Boston: Little, Brown.

GILBREATH, ALICE THOMPSON. 1986. *The Great Barrier Reef: A Treasure in the Sea.* Minneapolis, MN: Dillon Press.

GLASER, MICHAEL. 1983. *Does Anyone Know Where a Hermit Crab Goes?* Fiskdale, MA: Knickerbocker Publishing Co.

GUCCIONE, LESLIE. 1991. *Nobody Listens to Me.* New York: Scholastic.

HIMMELMAN, JOHN. 1990. *Ibis: A True Whale Story.* New York: Scholastic.

HOLLENBECK, KATHLEEN. 1996. *Lobster's Secret.* Washington, DC: Trudy Management Corp. and the Smithsonian Institute.

HOLLING, HOLLING C. 1957, 1990. *Pagoo.* Boston: Houghton Mifflin.

HULME, JOY. 1991. *Sea Squares.* New York: Hyperion Books for Children.

———. 1996. *Sea Sums.* New York: Hyperion Books for Children.

IPCAR, DAHLOV. 1962. *Lobsterman.* Camden, ME: Down East Books.

JOHNSON, SYLVIA. 1981. *Penguins.* Minneapolis, MN: Lerner Publications.

———. 1984. *Coral Reefs.* Minneapolis, MN: Lerner Publications.

JONES, DOROTHY, and SARGENT, RUTH. 1992. *The Original Biography of Abbie Burgess, Lighthouse Heroine.* Peaks Island, ME: Ruth S. Sargent.

KESSELMAN, WENDY, and RONALD HIMLER. 1995. *Sand in My Shoes.* New York: Hyperion Books for Children.

KRASKE, ROBERT. 1995. *The Voyager's Stone: The Adventures of a Message Carrying Bottle Adrift on the Ocean Sea.* New York: Orchard Books.

LIONNI, LEO. 1963. *Swimmy.* New York: Knopf Books for Young Readers.

MACQUITTY, MIRANDA. 1992. *Shark.* New York: Knopf Books for Young Readers.

MALNIG, ANITA. 1985. *Where the Waves Break: Life at the Edge of the Sea.* Minneapolis, MN: Carolrhoda Books.

McCLOSKEY, ROBERT. 1963. *Burt Dow: Deep-Water Man.* New York: Viking Children's Books.

McDONALD, MEGAN. 1990. *Is This a House for Hermit Crab?* New York: Orchard Books.

McHargue, Georgess. 1973. *The Mermaid and the Whale.* New York: Holt, Rinehart & Winston.

McMillan, Bruce. 1977. *Finest Kind O' Day: Lobstering in Maine.* New York: Lippincott Children's Books.

———. 1992. *Going on a Whale Watch.* New York: Scholastic.

———. 1993. *A Beach for the Birds.* Boston: Houghton Mifflin.

———. 1993. *Penguins at Home: Gentoos of Antartica.* Boston: Houghton Mifflin.

———. 1995. *Summer Ice: Life Along the Antarctic Peninsula.* Boston: Houghton Mifflin.

Milton, Joyce. 1989. *Whales: The Gentle Giants.* New York: Random House Books for Young Readers.

Nixon, Hershell, and Joan Lowery Nixon. 1983. *Land Under the Sea.* New York: Dodd, Mead.

Orr, Katherine. 1984. *Shelley.* London: Macmillan Caribbean.

———. 1985. *Leroy the Lobster.* London: Macmillan Caribbean.

Pallotta, Jerry. 1989. *The Ocean Alphabet Book.* Watertown, MA: Charlesbridge Publishing.

———. 1990. *Going Lobstering.* Watertown, MA: Charlesbridge Publishing.

———. 1991. *The Underwater Alphabet Book.* Watertown, MA: Charlesbridge Publishing.

Patent, Dorothy Henshaw. 1993. *Looking at Penguins.* New York: Holiday House.

Payne, Roger. *Songs of the Humpback Whale.* Recording, Columbia ST-620 (disc) or 4XT-620 (cassette).

Pope, Joyce. 1990. *Seashores.* Mahwah, NJ: Troll Associates.

Poucet, S. 1995. *Antarctic Encounter: Destination South Georgia.* New York: Simon and Schuster.

Rabin, Staton. 1992. *Monster Myths: The Truth About Water Monsters.* New York: Franklin Watts.

Reiser, Lynn. 1996. *Beach Feet.* New York: Greenwillow Books.

Robinson, Jane. 1992. *The Whale in Lowell's Cove.* Camden, ME: Down East Books.

Roop, Peter, and Connie Roop. 1985. *Keep the Lights Burning, Abbie.* Minneapolis, MN: Carolrhoda Books.

RYLANT, CYNTHIA. 1996. *The Whales.* New York: Scholastic.

SARGENT, WILLIAM. 1991. *Night Reef: Dusk to Dawn on a Coral Reef.* New York: Franklin Watts.

SEGALOFF, NAT, and PAUL ERICKSON. 1991. *A Reef Comes to Life: Creating an Undersea Exhibit.* New York: Franklin Watts.

SERVER, LEE. 1990. *World of Nature Sharks.* New York: Gallery Books.

SHELDON, DYAN. 1991. *The Whales' Song.* New York: Dial Books for Young Readers.

SIMON, SEYMOUR. 1987. *Icebergs and Glaciers.* New York: Morrow Junior Books.

SMITH, ROLAND. 1990. *Sea Otter Rescue: The Aftermath of an Oil Spill.* New York: Cobblehill Books.

SMYTH, KAREN. 1986. *Crystal: The Story of a Real Baby Whale.* Camden, ME: Down East Books.

SNEDDEN, ROBERT. 1993. *What Is a Fish?* San Francisco: Sierra Club Books for Children.

SPEDDEN, DAISY. 1994. *Polar the Titanic Bear.* Boston: Little, Brown.

STEIG, WILLIAM. 1971. *Amos and Boris.* New York: Farrar, Straus & Giroux.

STOLTZ, MARY. 1985. *Night of Ghosts and Hermits: Nocturnal Life on the Seashore.* San Diego: Harcourt Brace Juvenile Books.

TANAKA, SHELLEY. 1996. *On Board the* Titanic. Toronto, Ontario: Hyperion/Madison Press.

TAYLOR, BARBARA. 1992. *Look Closer: Coral Reef.* New York: Dorling Kindersley.

TAYNTOR, ELIZABETH, PAUL ERICKSON, and LES KAUFMAN. 1986. *Dive to the Coral Reefs.* New York: Crown Publishers.

WATERS, JOHN. 1991. *Watching Whales.* New York: Cobblehill Books.

———. 1994. *Deep-Sea Vents: Living Worlds Without Sun.* New York: Cobblehill Books.

WELLER, FRANCES WARD. 1991. *I Wonder If I'll See a Whale.* New York: Philomel Books.

WELLS, ROBERT. 1993. *Is a Blue Whale the Biggest Thing There Is?* Morton Grove, IL: Albert Whitman & Co.

WELLS, SUE. 1994. *Make Your Own Coral Reef.* New York: Lodestar Books.

YOLEN, JANE. 1968. *Greyling.* New York: World Publishing.

Final Thoughts

Recently, the preliminary results were released of the largest international comparative study ever undertaken of mathematics and science education, *Third International Mathematics and Science Study,* also called *TIMSS* (National Research Council 1996). U. S. children in grades 4, 9, and 12 were tested and compared to students from forty other countries. An in-depth survey was also conducted of the curricula, teaching methods, and school cultures of six countries that researchers felt would represent a cross-section of all the countries in the study: France, Japan, Norway, Spain, Switzerland, and the United States (*Study of Mathematics and Science Opportunities,* 1996).

In the U. S. it was found that there is a tendency to address a given science topic repeatedly over a period of several grades, resulting in a course of study that is "a mile wide and an inch deep." Textbooks, as noted earlier, may contribute to this problem since they often cover extensive material in a cursory fashion in order to be all-inclusive. Trade books, on the other hand, allow students to explore fewer topics of interest in-depth.

Analyzing the data from these two studies will keep educational researchers busy at least through 1998, but there are some early indicators that suggest that countries with comprehensive, coherent goals of what should be expected of all students did better than those without a focused vision. This corresponds to current reform movements in the United States that promote building local curriculum, instruction, and assessment on a foundation of rigorous state and national science and mathematics standards.

After years of collaboration among classroom teachers, education administrators, scientists, engineers, businesspeople, and policy makers, both the American Association for the Advancement of Science and the National Research Council have released national guidelines for achieving high standards in science education: *Science for All Americans* (1990), the AAAS *Benchmarks for Science Literacy* (1993), and the National Research Council's *National Science Education Standards* (1996). Several states, as well as individual school districts, have also issued recommended or mandatory science standards. These documents are designed to assist educators (including school boards, staff developers, parent groups, curriculum committees, teachers, and administrators) in developing science curriculum and classroom practices that will consistently move students toward higher achievement. As the Maine Mathematics and Science Alliance pointed out in 1996, these standards allow school districts flexibility in the design and implementation of science curricula, much like building codes that set safety and performance standards for new construction while allowing for individualized style and approach. By posing questions about teaching style and content and by providing examples of how others teach science, the standards help teachers reflect on their own teaching to see if it is challenging, engaging, and appropriate for their learners.

How does a classroom teacher respond to all this helpful advice from national, state, and local advisors? In many instances, the standards just codify the common sense, good practices, and high standards that exemplary teachers have been using all along. Elementary teachers have long known what educational research is substantiating: that children learn best through active engagement. In the new "inquiry science," innovative teachers try to provide activities that allow students to explore their world in a disciplined fashion, while encouraging creativity, initiative, and risk taking.

Among the recommendations is the idea that "Less is better." Rather than watering down the curriculum, this means exploring fewer topics in greater depth, using a variety of methods, so that children emerge with a deep understanding rather than just memorizing vocabulary words or parroting back facts. This philosophy reflects the realization that it takes time and reinforcement in order to incorporate important ideas into one's personal knowledge base. I believe it also legitimizes the use of trade books in preference to a science textbook, so that you can explore a topic in detail and through several authors' perspectives.

The National Education Standards from the National Research Council place less emphasis on knowing scientific facts and information and more emphasis on understanding scientific concepts and developing inquiry skills—understanding the "big ideas." Getting the answer is not an end in itself; it is less important than applying the results of an experiment to scientific arguments and explanation—a point well made in the 1996 newsletter, *Making a Difference.* Along the lines of this philosophy, teachers may decide to introduce scientific terms in conjunction with experiences, rather than asking students to write definitions as a precursor to studying a topic.

By starting with an overarching question, issue, or problem raised by reading a trade book, the teacher can explore what students already know (or think they know) about a topic. This also allows the teacher to identify and address misconceptions. If there are misconceptions, you can try to dispel them by teaching the correct concepts in several different ways (and, although it doesn't always convince students, telling them if their preconceptions are flawed). By providing questions before answers, you encourage students to think on their own and not merely wait for the teacher to dispense knowledge from above.

Combining theme-based, hands-on science and children's literature supports many of the learning goals of the new standards that recommend students explore a variety of learning experiences that relate to previous knowledge, their experiences, or their interests. Theme-based units use hands-on activities in ways that build connections to scientific concepts. They focus on thinking, reasoning, and making sense of what they're doing. Working together at least part of the time, students can trade ideas, share tasks, and prepare classroom presentations. Students have an opportunity to experiment with different approaches as they work toward making their own discoveries.

In addition to engaging students in hands-on activities and reading books, it's important to provide time for children to reflect on what they have learned. Class discussions, sharing ideas with a partner, journal writing or other writing, and presenting projects that demonstrate understanding of concepts, beyond just "show and tell," are some ways teachers encourage reflection.

Besides traditional testing, student assessment may incorporate creating portfolios of their work, such as science projects and written papers; videotapes of oral presentations to other students, parents, or the community; graphs, stories, songs, models, letters to the editor, skits, debates, field guides, crossword puzzles, class newspapers, book reviews, advertisements, charades, inventions, cartoons, games, picture dictionaries, slide shows, posters, timelines, and so on. Because it is important for all children to master science, assessments need to include some opportunities for every student to demonstrate what he or she has learned.

While local, state, and national standards may use different language, they all have a similar goal: to produce students who can solve problems, collaborate, and communicate. If you dropped in on an elementary classroom engaged in exemplary science, you would notice that it

- connects science to the outside world
- integrates other subject areas whenever possible
- provides experiential and active learning
- encourages cooperative learning when appropriate

- emphasizes reasoning and problem solving over memorization of facts

- strives to cover a few fundamental science concepts in-depth, rather than trying to cover many science topics superficially

- expects students to demonstrate knowledge in a variety of ways

- incorporates a variety of educational materials, which may include trade books, hands-on manipulatives, and technology, such as computers, calculators, satellite images, CD-ROMs, and the like.

These ideas are derived from *Maine's Curriculum Framework for Mathematics and Science,* developed in 1996 by the Maine Mathematics and Science Alliance, and from national science standards.

In *doing* science, not just observing science, students become "principal investigators" engaged in their own research. This approach may lead them beyond what the teacher expects of them. By reasoning, questioning, collecting data both through a combination of their own investigations and reading the works of others, students accumulate the information to make their own judgments. As they compare information from several sources, students also begin to realize that even scientists often disagree about data and theories.

What makes science so exciting—and this is important for students to understand—is that the answers, in many cases, aren't already known. Scientists learn by asking questions, exploring new avenues, making connections, making mistakes, and arriving at conclusions that inevitably generate new questions. At some point, too, these young people may contribute to the expanding body of knowledge in science. By training students to think like scientists, classroom teachers are freed from being the "givers of knowledge." Instead they become facilitators who guide the learning experience and, as learners along with their students, can also seek answers to their own questions along the way. Just like reading a good book, the outcome of a scientific exploration isn't necessarily known until the last page.

Works Cited

American Association for the Advancement of Science. 1990. *Science for All Americans.* New York: Oxford University Press.

American Association for the Advancement of Science. 1993. *Benchmarks for Science Literacy.* New York: Oxford University Press.

Armbruster, Bonnie. 1993. "Science and Reading." *The Reading Teacher* 46(4): 346–47.

Atwater, Mary M. 1995. "The Cross-Curricular Classroom." *Science Scope* (October): 42–45.

Ballard, M., and M. Pandya. 1990. *Essential Learnings in Environmental Education: A Database for Building Activities and Programs.* Trot, OH: North American Association for Environmental Education.

Bosma, B. 1992. "The Voice of Learning: Teacher, Child, and Text." In *Using Nonfiction Trade Books in the Elementary Classroom: From Ants to Zeppelins,* edited by Evelyn B. Freeman and Diane Goetz Person. Urbana, IL: National Council of Teachers of English.

Brearton, Mary Ann, Field Services Coordinator, Project 2061, AAAS. Personal communication, 4 September 1996.

Breger, Debra. 1995. "The Inquiry Paper." *Science Scope* (October): 27–31.

Commission on Maine's Common Core of Learning. 1990. *Maine's Common Core of Learning: An Investment in Maine's Future.* Augusta, ME: Maine Department of Education.

Dickens, Eleanor, ed. 1996. *Maine's Curriculum Framework in Mathematics and Science.* Augusta, ME: Maine Mathematics and Science Alliance.

Dowd, F. 1992. "Trends and Evaluative Criteria of Informational Books for Children." In *Using Nonfiction Trade Books in the Elementary*

Classroom: From Ants to Zeppelins, edited by Evelyn B. Freeman and Diane Goetz Person. Urbana, IL: National Council of Teachers of English.

EARLE, SYLVIA. 1995. *Sea Change*. New York: GP Putnam's Sons.

EGGERTON, SUSAN. 1996. "Balancing Science and Sentiment: The Portrayal of Nature and the Environment in Children's Literature." *Science and Children* (March): 20–23.

EISELEY, LOREN. 1957. *The Immense Journey*. New York: Random.

ELLEMAN, B. 1992. "The Nonfiction Scene: What's Happening?" In *Using Nonfiction Trade Books in the Elementary Classroom: From Ants to Zeppelins*, edited by Evelyn B. Freeman and Diane Goetz Person. Urbana, IL: National Council of Teachers of English.

FREEDMAN, R. 1992. "Fact or Fiction?" In *Using Nonfiction Trade Books in the Elementary Classroom: From Ants to Zeppelins*, edited by Evelyn B. Freeman and Diane Goetz Person. Urbana, IL: National Council of Teachers of English.

LAPP, D., and J. Flood. 1992. "Literature in the Science Program." In *Fact and Fiction: Literature Across the Curriculum*, edited by Bernice E. Cullinan. Newark, NJ: International Reading Association.

LAUBER, PATRICIA. 1992. "The Evolution of a Science Writer." In *Using Nonfiction Trade Books in the Elementary Classroom: From Ants to Zeppelins*, edited by Evelyn B. Freeman and Diane Goetz Person. Urbana, IL: National Council of Teachers of English.

MARINE CONSERVATON INITIATIVE, THE. 1996. *Presentation of Findings from a Nationwide Survey and Focus Groups*. Washington, DC: The Mellman Group.

MECHLING, K., and L. Kepler. 1991. "Start with Science." *Instructor* (March).

MILLER, KENNETH, STANLEY STEINER, and CAROLYN LARSON. 1996. "Strategies for Science Learning." *Science and Children* (March): 24–27.

NATIONAL RESEARCH COUNCIL. 1996. *Mathematics and Science Education Around the World; What Can We Learn from the Survey of Mathematics and Science Opportunities (SMSO) and the Third International Mathematics and Science Study (TIMSS)*. Washington, DC: National Academy Press.

NATIONAL RESEARCH COUNCIL. 1996. *National Science Education Standards*. Washington, DC: National Academy Press.

STIFFLER, LEE ANNE. 1992. "A Solution in the Shelves." *Science and Children* (March): 17.

TUCKER, GEORGIA, ed. 1996. "Science Teaching Standards from the National Academy of Sciences." *Making a Difference: Newsletter of the New York Statewide Systemic Initiative* 2(7): 2–5.